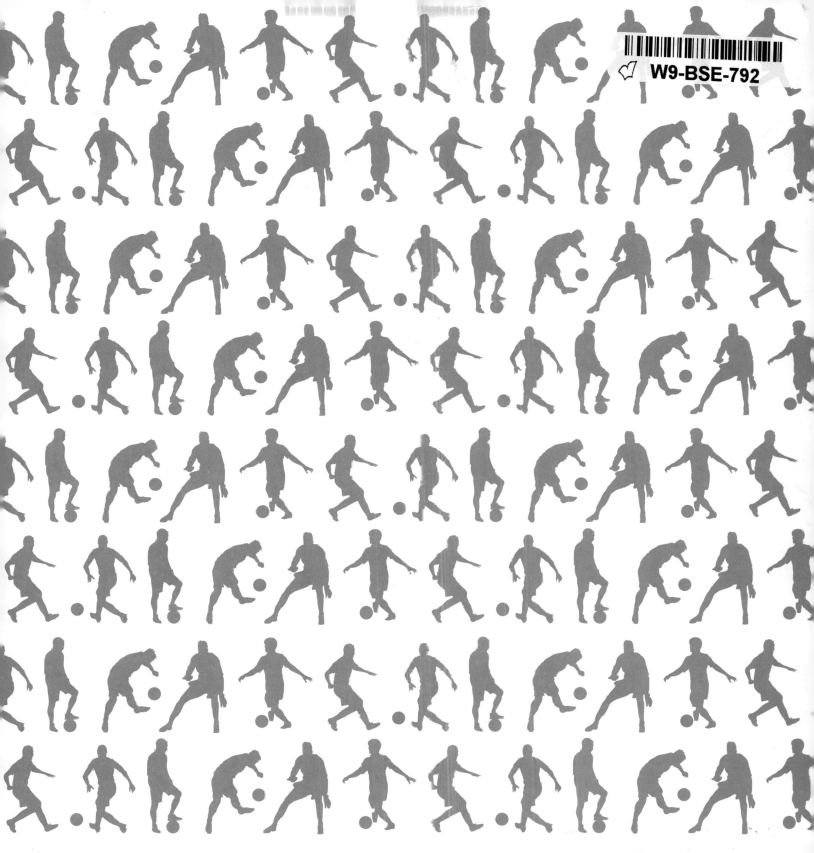

W9-BSE-792

SOCCER

THE COMPLETE
QUICK-LOOK GUIDE
— TO THE GAME OF —
SOCCER

GABRIELA SCOLIK & TEAM

ILLUSTRATIONS KARIN DREHER

weldon**owen**

learn the rules

play the game

watch the game

know the facts

Know the Score!

Around the world, soccer (or football, or fussball, or the most important thing in the universe) is king. Whether you can quote chapter and verse on every World Cup victory since 1930 (#153) and have opinions about how the game was played in 11th-century England (#145) or just you're curious about what exactly the offsides rule is (#034), this book is for you. Packed with information you can use this very weekend in your local park—amazing everyone with your fancy footwork (#054)—or at least avoid making any embarrassing mistakes (#069). After the game, amaze everyone at the pub with your arcane knowledge of bizarre soccer injuries (#199) and whether it's a good idea to swear if you're a member of the Vatican's official team (#216). Spoiler alert—it's not a good idea.

To quote German soccer legend Sepp Herberger (#169), "The ball is round, the game lasts 90 minutes, everything else is pure theory."

And what if you're more a fan than a player? The sport of soccer is particularly welcoming to its fans, who have a rich history of colorful gear (#115) and offbeat antics (#121). Step-by-step tutorials will teach you how to tie-dye a T-shirt in your team's colors (#128), sport an authentic on-field hairdo (#203), and even deck out your sweet soccer ride (#122). Just don't engage in any epic acts of hooliganism (#137).

A quick note about money: Since so much of the big-money stats come out of Europe (#189) and the sums are similar enough, we've kept the figures in euros instead of converting to dollars.

Here's a little roadmap to help you use the handy features you'll find in this book. Everything is presented in a highly graphic illustrated format, and, in most cases, the pictures tell the story. Every so often, however, it may be useful to understand how special information is portrayed.

ARROWS
Arrows indicate direction of movement.
Yellow arrow = where the player is going

Blue arrow = where the ball is going

111 understand the language of the linesman

034 see offsides
Offside position at the opposite side of the playing field

034 see offsides
Offside position near the linesman

034 see offsides
Offside

034 see offsides
Offside position in the middle of the playing field

026 watch a throw-in
Throw-in

C57 see the inner side-footed kick

Normal passes are mostly played with the inside of your foot to achieve the highest passing accuracy.

The standing leg points in the passing direction.

The free leg is fixed at the joint.

The foot posture determines the direction of the kick.

CROSS-REFERENCES
Sometimes one thing leads to the next. Follow the numbers to find more or additional information or related topics elsewhere in the book. The numbers' colored circles refer to the chapter where you can find the entry.

000 learn the rules

000 watch the game

000 play the game

000 know the facts

ZOOMS
Here you can find more detailed information within a larger picture. You might get a closer look at the position of the player or more instructions on the angle of the maneuver.

GENDER-INCLUSIVE LANGUAGE It should go without saying that whenever we speak of players, trainers, or referees, the tip or regulation applies across the gender spectrum, even in cases where male, female, or neutral pronouns are used. Excellence in sports doesn't discriminate, and neither does this book.

learn
the rules

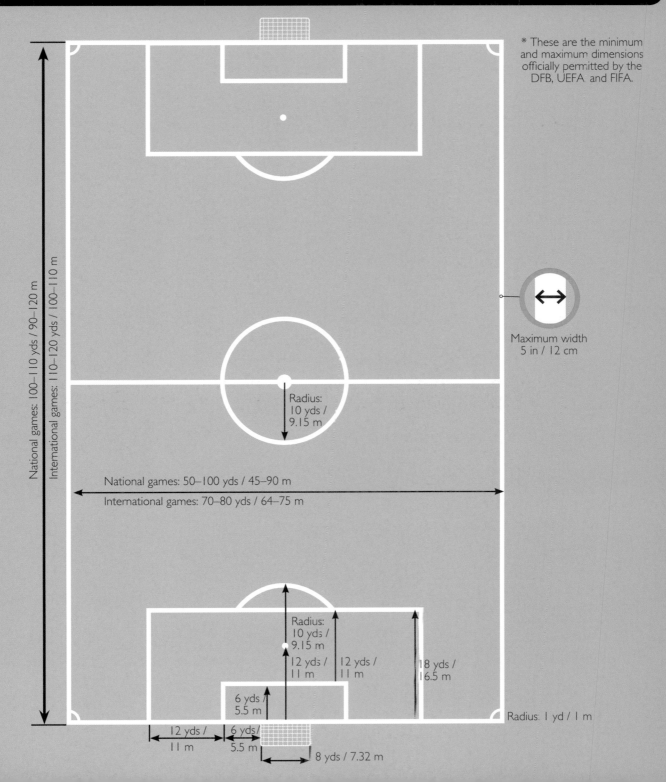

* These are the minimum and maximum dimensions officially permitted by the DFB, UEFA and FIFA.

National games: 100–110 yds / 90–120 m

International games: 110–120 yds / 100–110 m

Maximum width
5 in / 12 cm

Radius:
10 yds /
9.15 m

National games: 50–100 yds / 45–90 m

International games: 70–80 yds / 64–75 m

Radius:
10 yds /
9.15 m

12 yds /
11 m

12 yds /
11 m

18 yds /
16.5 m

6 yds /
5.5 m

Radius: 1 yd / 1 m

12 yds /
11 m

6 yds /
5.5 m

8 yds / 7.32 m

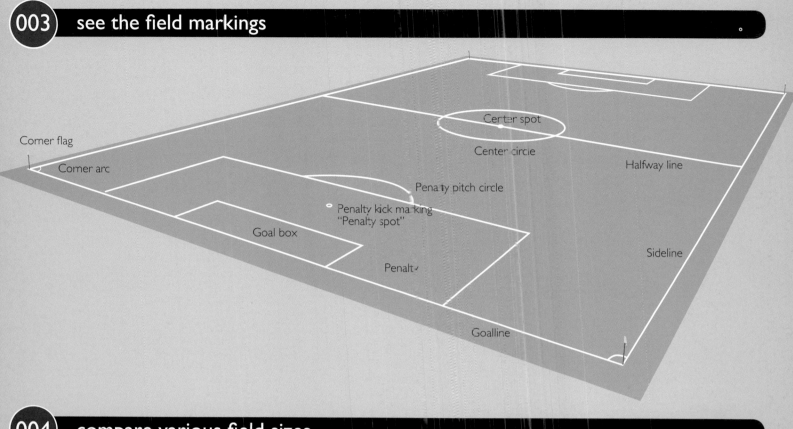

Corner flag

Corner arc

Goal box

Penalty kick marking
"Penalty spot"

Penalty pitch circle

Penalt...

Center spot

Center circle

Halfway line

Sideline

Goalline

004   compare various field sizes

The playing field is a rectangular field that is flat and obstacle-free. Normally the flooring material is grass;
more rarely, games are played on artificial lawns. Youth teams play on smaller fields.

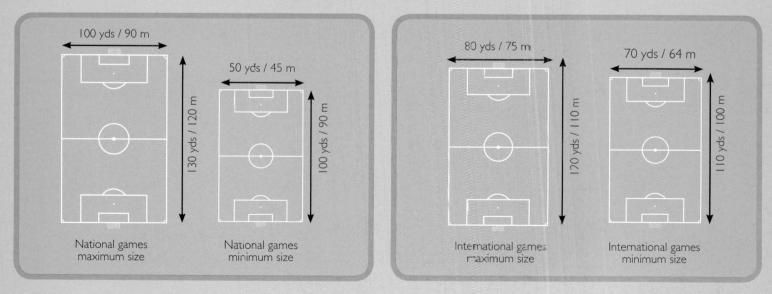

100 yds / 90 m

130 yds / 120 m

National games
maximum size

50 yds / 45 m

100 yds / 90 m

National games
minimum size

80 yds / 75 m

120 yds / 110 m

International games
maximum size

70 yds / 64 m

110 yds / 100 m

International games
minimum size

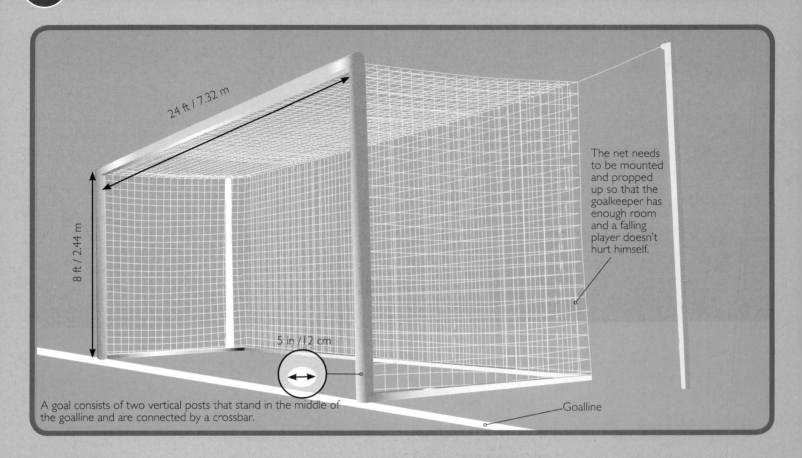

24 ft / 7.32 m

8 ft / 2.44 m

5 in / 12 cm

The net needs to be mounted and propped up so that the goalkeeper has enough room and a falling player doesn't hurt himself.

Goalline

A goal consists of two vertical posts that stand in the middle of the goalline and are connected by a crossbar.

The ball must be round and made of leather or another suitable material.

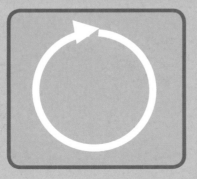

Its circumference must be at least 27 in / 68.5 cm and at most 27.5 in / 70 cm.

At the start of the game the ball must weigh at least 14.5 oz / 410 g; at most 15.9 oz / 450 g.

The ball's pressure must be 8.7–15.9 psi / 0.6–1.1 bar or 600–1100 g/cm^2.

007 learn about teams

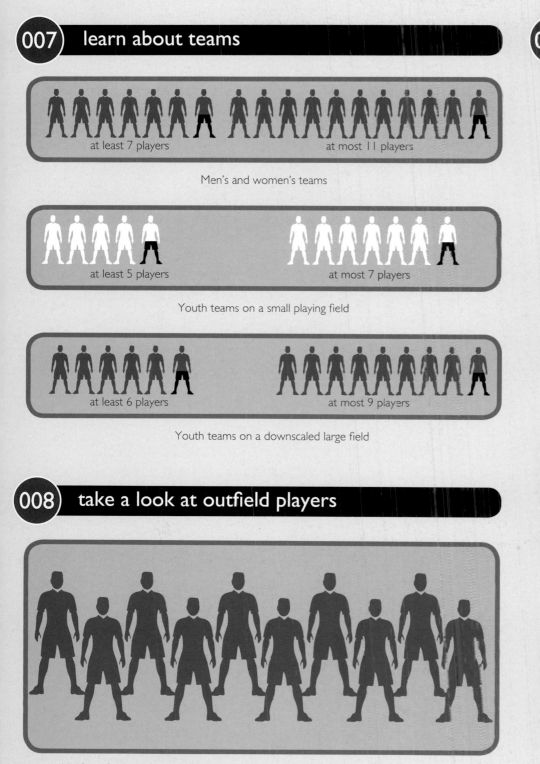

at least 7 players   at most 11 players

Men's and women's teams

at least 5 players   at most 7 players

Youth teams on a small playing field

at least 6 players   at most 9 players

Youth teams on a downscaled large field

008 take a look at outfield players

All 10 outfield players need to wear uniform shirts. The color of the goalkeeper's shirt needs to be distinguishable from that of the others including that of the referee.

009 see shirt colors

Professional teams wear a home and an away shirt, which differ greatly in terms of color.

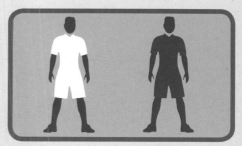

The team that is named first in the match title is allowed to wear home shirts.

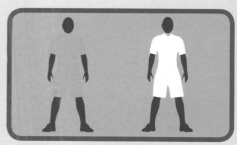

If the colors of the two teams are too similar the referee can demand wearing away shirts.

The shirt colors must be clearly distinguishable from those of the referee and the linesmen.

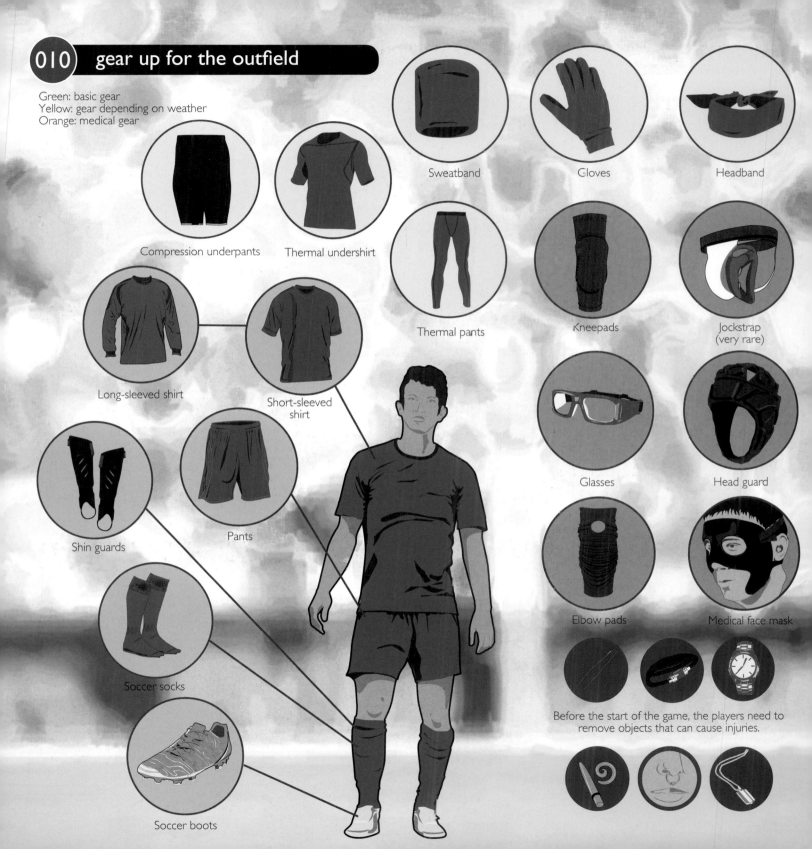

010 gear up for the outfield

Green: basic gear
Yellow: gear depending on weather
Orange: medical gear

Compression underpants

Thermal undershirt

Sweatband

Gloves

Headband

Long-sleeved shirt

Short-sleeved shirt

Thermal pants

Kneepads

Jockstrap (very rare)

Shin guards

Pants

Glasses

Head guard

Soccer socks

Elbow pads

Medical face mask

Before the start of the game, the players need to remove objects that can cause injuries.

Soccer boots

011 watch outfield players

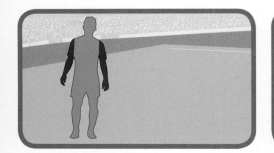

Outfield players can use their whole body during the game—except for their arms and hands.

Deliberately touching the ball with the arm or hand can lead to a penalty kick.

033 witness a penalty kick **029** get a free kick

012 follow the team captain

The captain must be marked with an armband.

He is the main contact of the referee.

013 get a goalkeeper

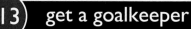

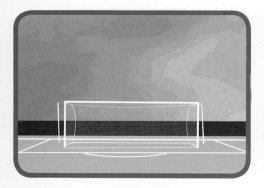

The game can't begin without the goalkeeper.

During an intermission an outfield player can take up the position of the goalkeeper, if the referee agrees to it. If the goalkeeper gets a red card, the substitute goalkeeper enters the game and one of the outfield players needs to leave the field as well.

gear up for goalkeeping

Green: basic gear
Yellow: gear depending on weather
Orange: medical gear

Kneepads

Jockstrap
(very rare)

Gloves

Sweatband

Headband

Glasses
(very rare)

Head guard

Thermal pants

Thermal undershirt

Elbow pads

Medical face mask

Long-sleeved shirt

Short-sleeved shirt

Before the start of the game, the goalkeeper needs
to remove objects that can cause injuries.

Pants

Long goalkeeper
pants

Shin guards

Soccer boots

Soccer socks

015   watch the goalkeeper work

The goalkeeper can use his hands inside the penalty box.

The goalkeeper can play the ball with his whole body in the penalty box.

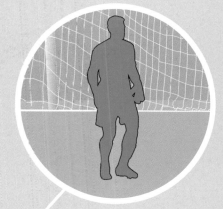

Outside of the penalty box the same rules apply to the goalkeeper as they do for the outfield players.

016 learn the back-pass rule

The goalkeeper may not use his hands if the ball is deliberately kicked back to him by foot or leg of his teammate.

The back-pass rule does not count for a header.

017 see the goalkeeper at penalty kick

The goalkeeper may only move on the goalline during a penalty kick.

033 witness a penalty kick

He may only move forward when the ball has been touched. Only then may the outfield players enter the penalty box.

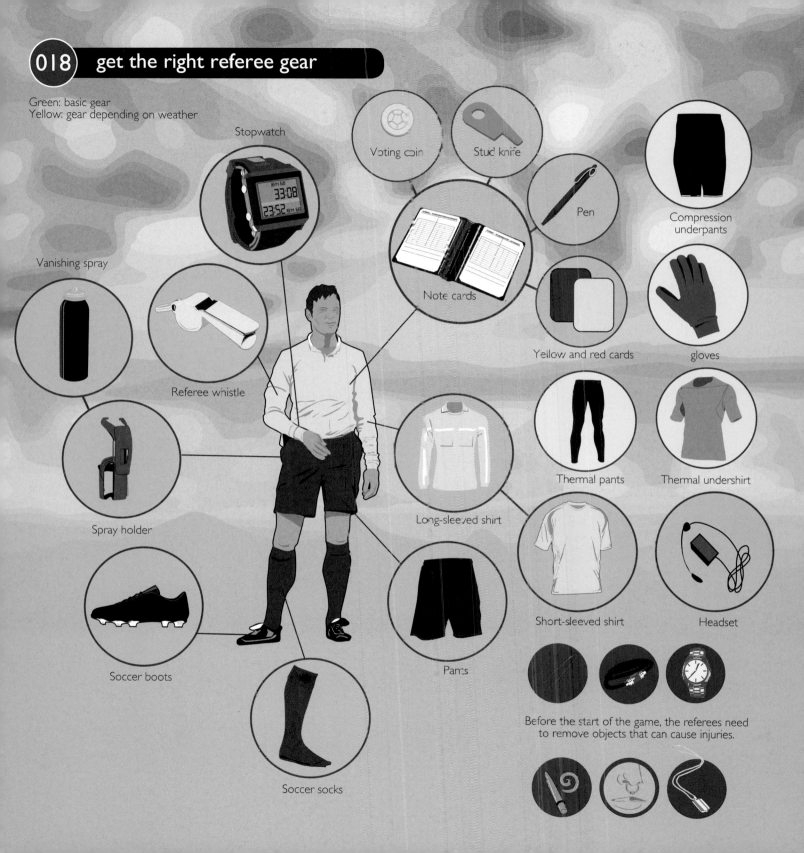

018 get the right referee gear

Green: basic gear
Yellow: gear depending on weather

Stopwatch

Voting coin

Stud knife

Pen

Compression underpants

Vanishing spray

Note cards

Yellow and red cards

gloves

Referee whistle

Thermal pants

Thermal undershirt

Spray holder

Long-sleeved shirt

Short-sleeved shirt

Headset

Soccer boots

Pants

Before the start of the game, the referees need to remove objects that can cause injuries.

Soccer socks

His decisions are factual decisions, which means they can't be refuted by the players.

His decisions are definite for both teams, even if they are wrong. This helps keep the game moving along.

Substitute players may not enter the field without his permission.

023   choose ends

The referee performs the coin-toss for the choice of ends.

He decides when a game is interrupted and when it continues.

024   watch the kickoff

The referee whistles to start and to stop the game.

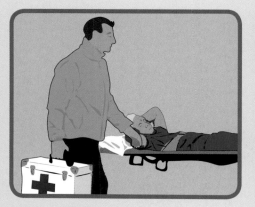

A drop ball can occur when a player injures himself without third party interference . . .

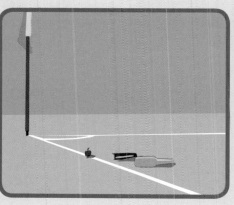

. . . or if there are objects on the field . . .

. . . or offences outside the playing field . . .

. . . or if the ball loses its form.

To execute a drop ball, the referee holds the ball up to his chest and drops it.

As soon as the ball hits the ground it can be played. Usually . . .

. . . two rivaling players are standing right next to the ref, and the ball is loosely kicked to the team that last had the ball.

A goal may not be scored from a drop ball. The ball must be touched at least twice (also by the same player)

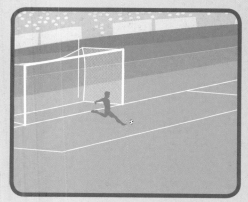

If the ball lands in the goal without having been touched a second time, a corner kick or goal kick is decided on.

The assistant referees help the referee at the sidelines.

understand the language of the linesman

They point out rule breaches to him.

Green: basic gear
Yellow: gear depending on weather

Compression Underpants

Long-sleeved shirt

Flags

Gloves

Thermal undershirt

Thermal pants

Pants

Short-sleeved shirt

Headset

Soccer socks

Soccer boots

Before the start of the game, the assistant referees need to remove objects that can cause injuries.

A game is 90 minutes long.

There are 15 minute breaks between the halftimes.

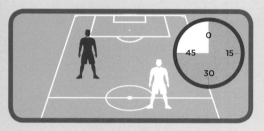

Both halftimes are 45 minutes long.

After the first halftime the playing sides are switched.

There can be added time at the end of a halftime, if there were longer interruptions.

The team captains and the referee perform the choice of ends before the game begins.

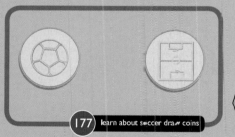

177 learn about soccer draw coins

The players decide on heads or tails, . . .

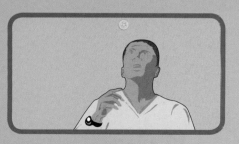

. . . the referee tosses the coin . . .

. . . and the winner may decide which goal his team gets to play on first

The other team performs the kickoff.

024 watch the kickoff

The match starts or continues with the kickoff.

It takes place at the start of a halftime, at the start of an overtime, and after a goal.

The kickoff is executed by two players of a team.

025 handle a time out

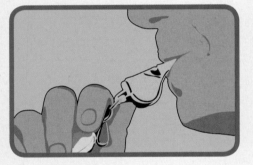

A time out is announced by the whistle of the referee . . .

. . . or after a goal is scored.

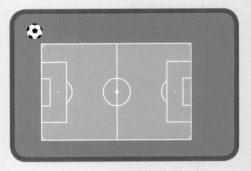

The game is also interrupted if the ball is outside the playing field.

026 watch a throw-in

If the ball ends up completely on the other side of the sidelines . . .

. . . it is important which player touched the ball last.

The respective other team can then execute the throw-in.

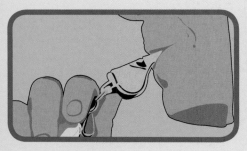

The game starts after the referee whistles.

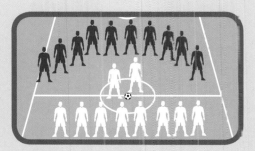

All players need to be on their respective sides.

The team that doesn't kick off may not be standing in the center circle during the starting whistle.

The ref whistles after a foul and announces a free kick.

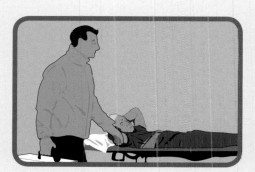

The game is also interrupted when a player is injured.

And the game is also stopped after a handball, a free kick (or penalty kick) follows.

Both feet need to be behind the sideline.

The player must throw the ball with both hands from behind his head.

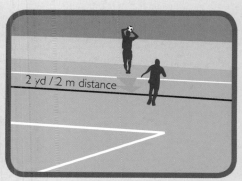

His teammates must keep a minimum 2 yds / 2 m distance.

get a goal kick

If the rival team plays the ball over the goalline from the right or left side of the goal . . .

. . . the goal keeper kicks off from any position within the goal box.

The ball is only back in the game after it's left the penalty area toward the playing field.

All rival players need to exit the penalty box during a goal kick.

A corner kick follows if, e.g., the attacking team shoots at the goal . . .

. . . and a defense player manoeuvers the ball behind the goalline . . .

. . . or if the offense kicks it past the goalline.

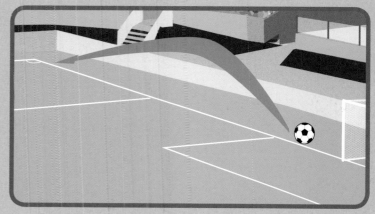

A corner kick is executed from the corner arc of the corner where the ball crossed the goalline.

The defense player must keep a 10 yd / 9.15 m distance to the corner arc.

Right

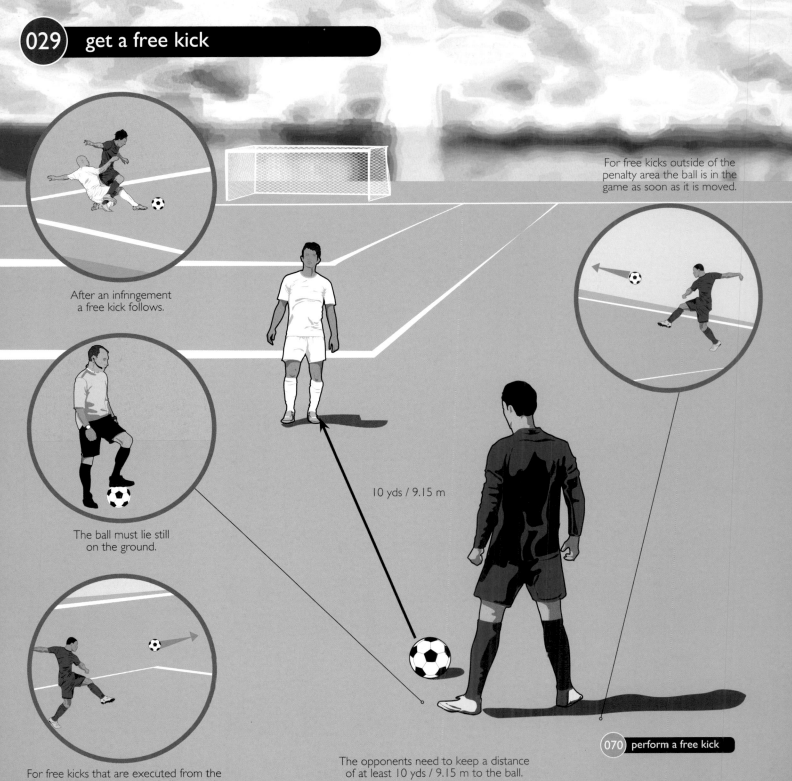

For free kicks outside of the penalty area the ball is in the game as soon as it is moved.

After an infringement a free kick follows.

The ball must lie still on the ground.

10 yds / 9.15 m

For free kicks that are executed from the team's own penalty box the ball enters the game as soon as it leaves the penalty area.

The opponents need to keep a distance of at least 10 yds / 9.15 m to the ball.

070 perform a free kick

062 understand fouls

The referee sprays a line for the wall.

071 set a defensive wall during free kick

A direct free kick is executed after a foul . . .

. . . or after a handball.

The players on the wall line may jump to block the ball.

A direct free kick is executed where the infringement took place. If it took place in the penalty area a penalty kick is executed.

Wall

033 witness a penalty kick

031 see an indirect free kick

034 see offsides

An indirect free kick follows after an offside . . .

063 know foul variants

. . . after dangerous play . . .

016 learn the back-pass rule

. . . after a breach of the back-pass rule . . .

. . . or after unsporting behavior like verbal abuse.

An indirect free kick is executed where the infringement took place.

042 score no goal after time out

An indirect free kick can also be played in the penalty area, even in the 6 yd / 5.5 m box, where it is executed from the line closest to the scene of the infringement.

A goal may not be scored directly from an indirect free kick. The ball must be touched at least two times first.

If a player commits a foul but the team that was fouled has a good chance at keeping the ball,
the referee can decide to let the game continue.

(063) know foul variants

witness a penalty kick

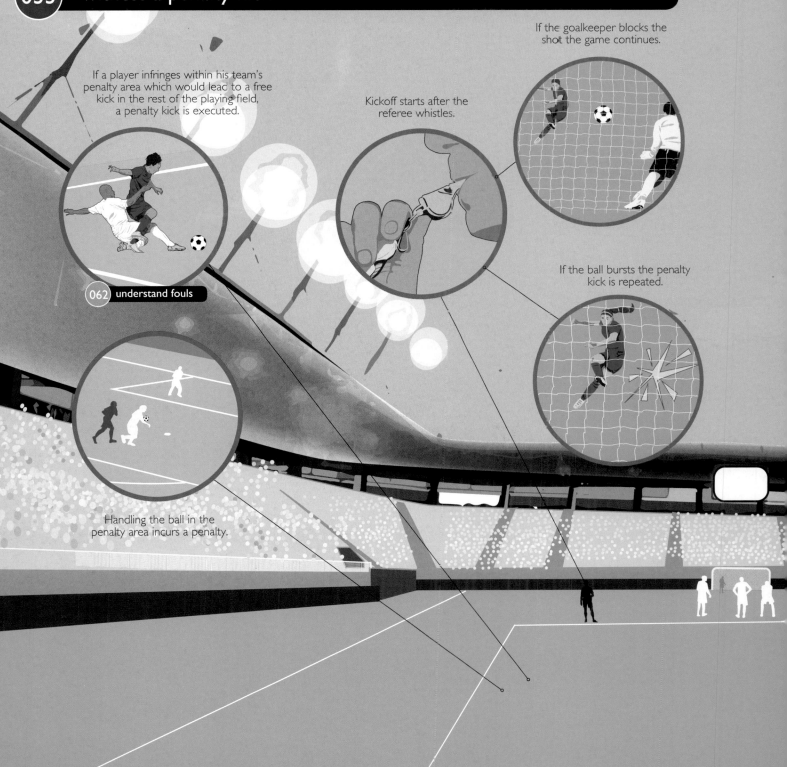

If a player infringes within his team's penalty area which would lead to a free kick in the rest of the playing field, a penalty kick is executed.

062 understand fouls

Kickoff starts after the referee whistles.

If the goalkeeper blocks the shot the game continues.

If the ball bursts the penalty kick is repeated.

Handling the ball in the penalty area incurs a penalty.

The ball lies on the penalty spot.

All players need to be 10 yds / 9.15 m
behind the penalty kick line and
outside of the penalty area.

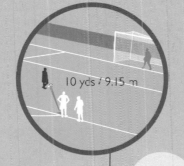

10 yds / 9.15 m

STOP

068 perform a penalty kick

017 see the goalkeeper at penalty kick

The goalkeeper may leave the goalline only after kickoff.

It is considered an offside if the attacking player, while he has possession of the ball and is passing to a teammate, . . .

. . . is located on the rivaling side, . . .

. . . is closer to the rivaling goalline than the ball, . . .

. . . or if he is closer to the rivaling goal with any part of his body (except for his arm or hand) that is suitable to score a goal than any player of the rivaling team.

Under these circumstances a player is also offside, if he blocks the goalkeeper's view of the scorer.

035 see an active offside

Active offside: A player without the ball is located offside and scores a goal in the direct course of the game. The goal doesn't count.

037 see no offside

No offside: The offending player is located on the same line as the rearmost defending player during a pass.

036 see a passive offside

Passive offside: A player is located offside but does not intervene in the course of the game. Offside is not punished.

There is no offside during corner kick and throw-in.

064 learn about diving or faking a foul

Faking a foul, also called diving

Tactical foul with the aim to disrupt the build-up of the opponent

2

Criticizing the referee, whining

Excessive goal celebration

1 Unsporting behavior
2 Protesting with words and actions
3 Repeated infringement
4 Slowing down the resumption of the game
5 Ignoring the compulsory distance during corner kick, free kick, or throw-in
6 (Re-)Entering the playing field without the referee's permission
7 Deliberately exiting the playing field without the referee's permission

5

Not keeping one's distance to the corner ball

4

Slowing down in order to create an advantage for the team

1–4 and 6 also apply to substitutes

understand a sending-off / red card

Yellow and red cards were first introduced during the 1970 World Cup in Mexico. The first yellow card was handed to Kurt Tschenscher at the opening game of Mexico versus the Soviet Union, the first red card was given to Carlos Caszely in 1974 at the World Cup group match of Chile versus Germany.

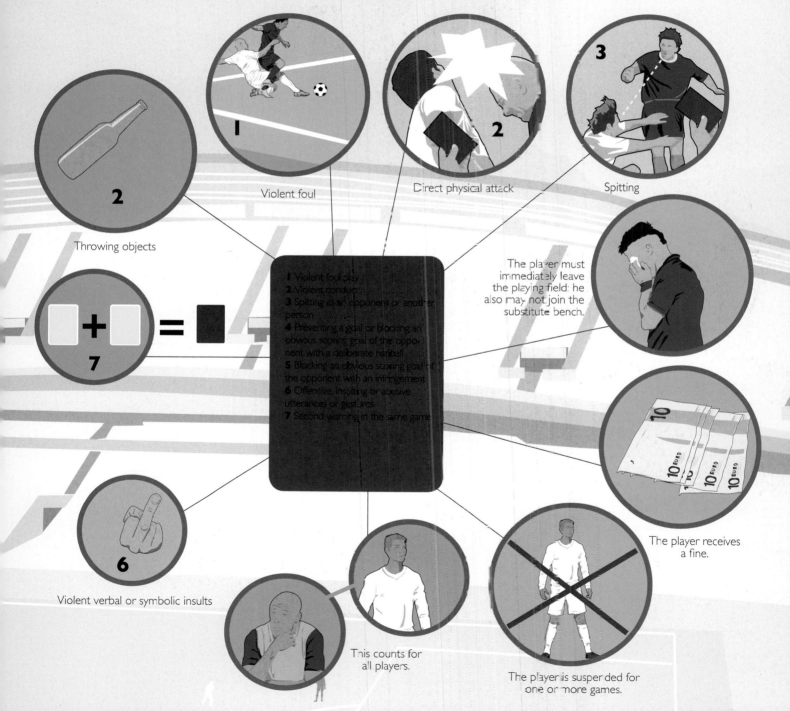

2

Throwing objects

Violent foul

Direct physical attack

Spitting

3

1 Violent foul play
2 Violent conduct
3 Spitting at an opponent or another person
4 Preventing a goal or blocking an obvious scoring goal of the opponent with a deliberate handball
5 Blocking an obvious scoring goal of the opponent with an infringement
6 Offensive, insulting or abusive utterances or gestures
7 Second warning in the same game

The player must immediately leave the playing field; he also may not join the substitute bench.

The player receives a fine.

6

Violent verbal or symbolic insults

This counts for all players.

The player is suspended for one or more games.

040 score a goal right

Not a goal . . .

Not a goal . . .

Not a goal . . .

GOAL!

A goal can be scored at any time during the running match.

041 score a goal after time out

024 watch the kickoff

027 get a goal kick

028 see a corner kick

033 witness a penalty kick

030 see a direct free kick

Direct goals are rarely scored after a kickoff, goal kick, or corner kick!

With a penalty kick

With a direct free kick

042 score no goal after time out

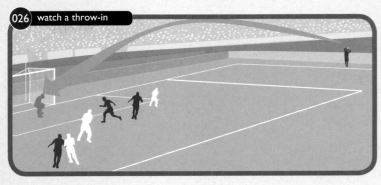

026 watch a throw-in

Throw-in without further contact with a player

031 see an indirect free kick

Indirect free kick, directly scoring a goal

043 understand substitution

Since 1967 an injured player can be substituted.

In 1967–1968 only one player per game was allowed to be subsituted.

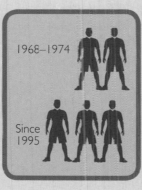

Since 1995 three players are allowed to be substituted.

1968–1974

Since 1995

Substituted players may not be substituted again.

0-3

In case of a substitution error the game is lost 0-3.

044 understand overtime

1 - 1

In a so-called "knock-out game" a five-minute break is added after a tie.

2 x 15 minutes are played during overtime.

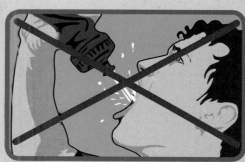

No halftime break

The sides are switched during halftime.

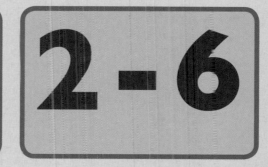

2 - 6

The team that scores the most goals wins. In case of a tie a penalty shootout is executed.

045 see a penalty shootout

045 see a penalty shootout

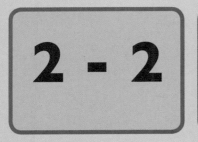

If the score is still tied after overtime, a penalty shootout is executed.

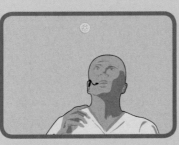

The referee decides with a coin toss which goal is shot at.

The game leaders each name the referee five scorers.

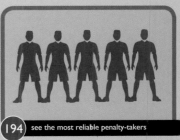

194 see the most reliable penalty-takers

Who feels good, confident, has nerves of steel, and is sure to score a penalty?

All players apart from the respective scorer and the goalkeepers need to stay within the center circle during the penalty shootout.

068 perform a penalty kick

The penalties are shot by turns.

The penalty shootout ends when a team is declared a certain winner because the deficit can't be made up (e.g. 4-2 after four penalties each).

Tie after five penalties: This procedure is repeated at one penalty each per team until a winner is declared. Even the goalkeepers have to shoot.

046 understand the away goals rule*

*at first and second leg games

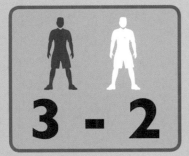

The blue team wins the home game 3-2.

The white team wins the second leg game at home 2-1.

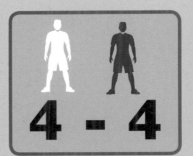

All goals are added up. In case of a tie the number of away goals decides.

The team that scores more away goals wins.

1864
Pants need to reach over the knee

1866
The offside rule is changed in order to make the game more fluid

1870
The team is limited to eleven players

1871
Only the goalkeeper is allowed to throw a handbal

1875
Introduction of the crossbar to goals

1877
Sending-off for violent foul play

1891
Introduction of the goal nets

1891
Penalty kick after a foul in the penalty area

1907
Offside is not possible on one's own side of the field

1925
The offside rule is changed again

1950
Introduction of compulsory footwear

1970
Yellow and red cards following infringements or unsporting behavior

1992
The back-pass rule is introduced

1993
Red card after a so-called "dangerous sliding tackle"

1995
Substitution by three substitute players

2013
Admission of goalline technology

play the game

It's best to receive or stop the ball with the inside of the foot, slightly lifting the foot. Tension is key!

Cushioning the impact of the ball.

Receiving the ball with the chest is technically not that easy but the most effective way to stop a high ball.

First you lean back slightly with your upper body . . .

Your chest should be in a tilted position and as wide as possible when the balls hits it.

. . . slightly pull back your shoulders, and bend your arms.

On impact, carefully pull your chest back, let the ball bounce of it, and secure it with your foot.

With a volley, you pass the ball in mid-air or directly take a shot at the goal (usually with your instep). If you succeed, it looks great and is risky for the goalkeeper. If you don't, it can be rather embarrassing. Don't lose heart!

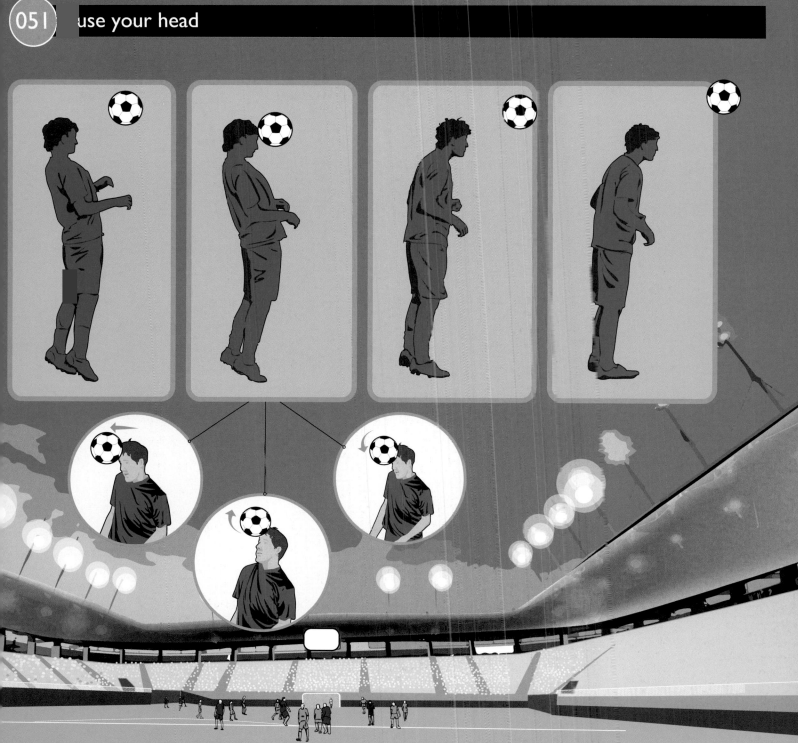

Swipe the ball with your head in the direction of your teammate in order to pass it on directly—this requires good timing!

Receiving the ball with the upper leg is rather rare. It usually happens while running and trying to push the ball directly into your own path. You can receive a midheight ball that is not kicked too fast with your upper leg by pulling your leg back a bit on impact.

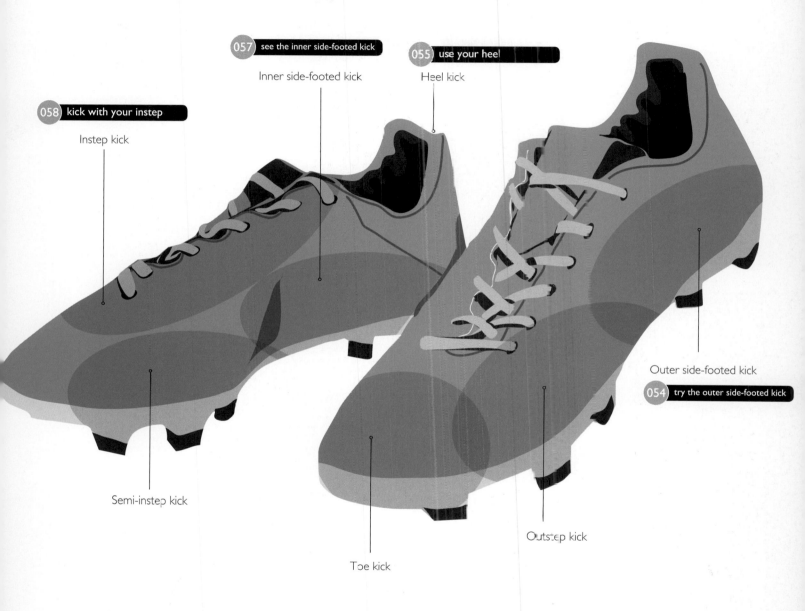

057 see the inner side-footed kick

Inner side-footed kick

055 use your heel

Heel kick

058 kick with your instep

Instep kick

Outer side-footed kick

054 try the outer side-footed kick

Semi-instep kick

Toe kick

Outstep kick

The ball is kicked in the desired direction with the outer side of the foot.

    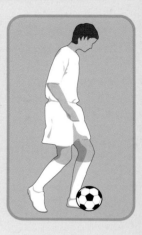

Pass the ball with your heel, if you want to surprise your opponent or want to play on quickly without turning around.

 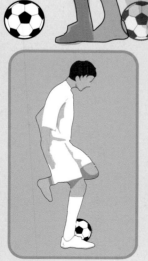   

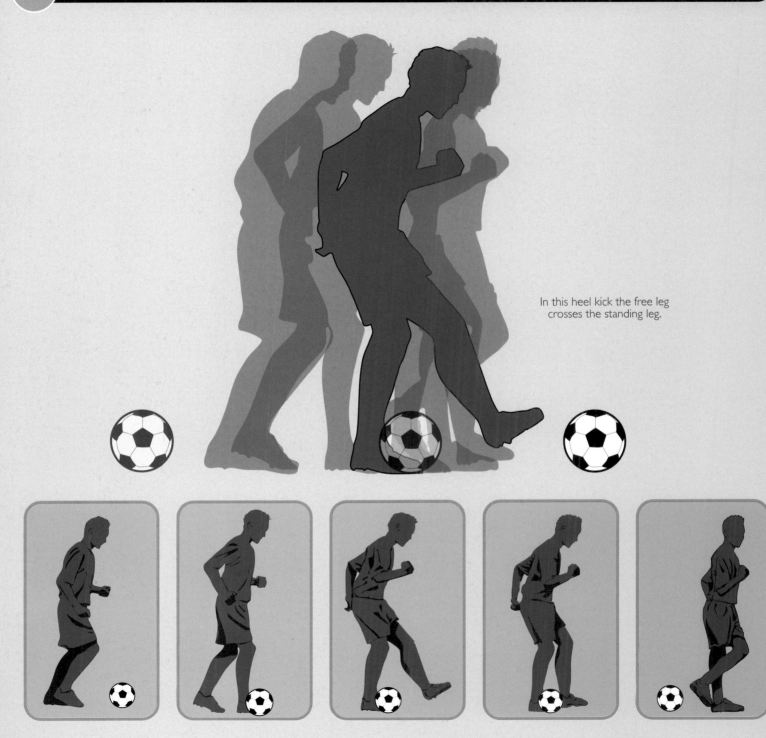

In this heel kick the free leg crosses the standing leg.

1

2

3

4

Normal passes are mostly played with the inside of your foot to achieve the highest passing accuracy.

The standing leg points in the passing direction.

The free leg is fixed at the joint.

The foot posture determines the direction of the kick.

The instep kick is used if you want to put a lot of force into it or kick especially far. The arm balances out the move diagonally to the shooting leg.

Kicking with a swerve creates friction between the ball's surface and the air.

The ball is kicked slightly from the side and starts to rotate.

The higher the ball spins the higher the rotation and curve trajectory.

(071) set a defensive wall during a free kick

Free kick scorers use the swerve to curl the ball around the defensive wall.

060 understand dribbling

To dribble means to get past the opponent on your own without passing the ball: keep the ball close to the foot, feel free to use tricks and—if possible—outsmart the opponent with speed.

061 keep the ball under control

You can also dribble in order to keep possession of the ball. Used as a tactic to irritate the opponent (and the audience).

Overly violent physical play is not allowed. Free kicks and additionally yellow or red cards are penalties for fouls. This is decided by the referee.

(038) understand a warning / yellow card

(039) understand a sending-off / red card

(033) witness a penalty kick

Fouls in the penalty box lead to a penalty kick.

Other fouls lead to direct free kicks.

030 see a direct free kick

If the referee overlooks a foul, this cannot be punished. Strongly objecting to misjudgements will not lead to free kicks or penalty kicks, but possibly a yellow card

Kicking the opponent

Tripping the opponent up

Pushing

Jumping at the opponent

Shoving

Beating

Pulling on the jersey top (or bottom)

Dangerous play (usually: leg too high)

Faking a foul is called diving. This can also lead to a yellow card.

The player tries to be awarded a free kick or a penalty kick.

038 understand a warning / yellow card

Letting yourself fall with arms and legs spread wide is (vaguely) similar to a flying swallow, hence the German term "Schwalbe" ("swallow") for diving.

A dive is usually accompanied by great indignation of the "fouled" player and a miraculously swift "recovery".

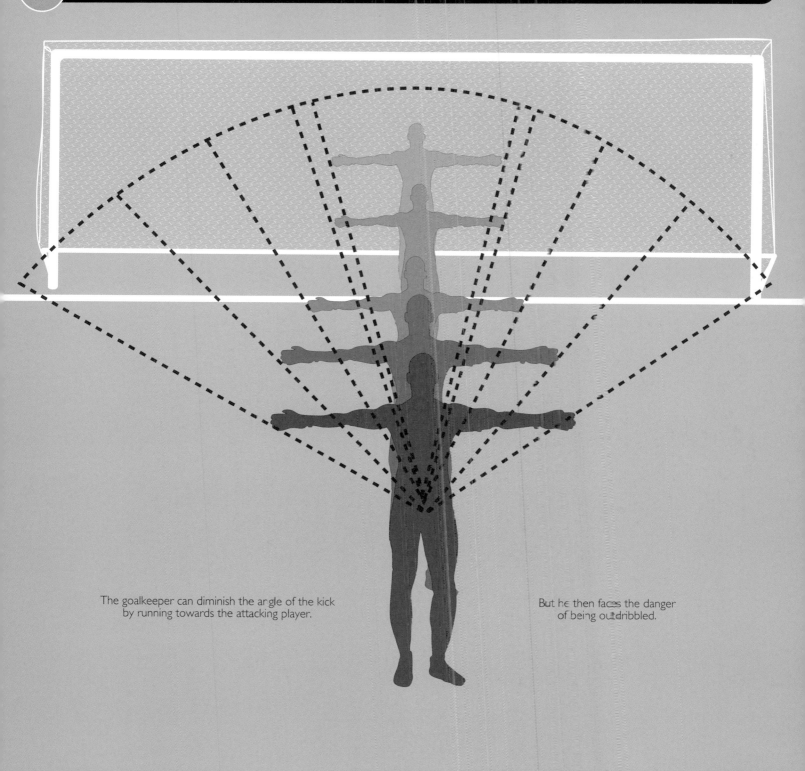

The goalkeeper can diminish the angle of the kick by running towards the attacking player.

But he then faces the danger of being outdribbled.

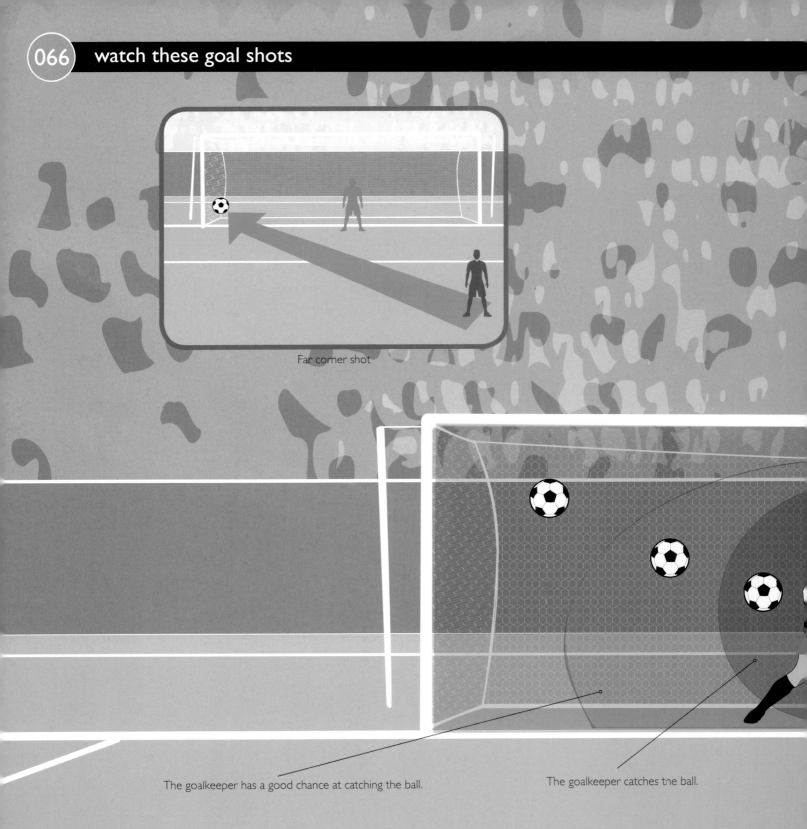

Far corner shot

The goalkeeper has a good chance at catching the ball.

The goalkeeper catches the ball.

Near corner shot

Only four or five goalkeepers worldwide can catch these bails.

High shot

Low shot

Hitting the crossbar

Placed shot

Hitting the corner of the goalpost

033 witness a penalty kick

About 80 percent of all penalty kicks are converted. The shot is almost always directed at the corners.

Safe penalty kicks

Can be easily held by the goalkeeper.

The goalkeeper often jumps off too early. But only veteran penalty takers can react fast enough.

Attack

Shot on goal

Rebound off the crossbar

The ball bounces off the goalkeeper
into the goal.

Defense

Defense

Goalkeeper

Offense

Offense

077 cross the ball

Own goals often occur
after crosses. The defense
inadvertently directs the ball
into their own goal.

(029) get a free kick

The referee determines where the free kick is executed.

The referee allows free kicks in front of the goal to be executed with a whistle.

The scorer is able to place the ball properly . . .

. . . shoots . . .

. . . and hopes to score.

(071) set a defensive wall during a free kick

029 get a free kick

During a free kick the players of the defending team form a wall in order to prevent a direct shot at the goal.

The referee marks the position of the wall and the ball with vanishing spray to prevent cheating.

The goalkeeper "conducts" the wall, telling his players where to position themselves.

When the referee allows the free kick both wall and goalkeeper should be ready.

059 give it a swerve

The scorer tries to shoot over, under, or around the wall.

Courageous players jump to intercept the ball.

072 understand which wall goes where

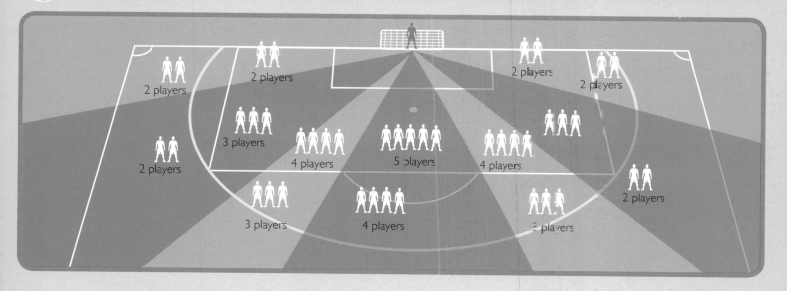

2 players

2 players

2 players

2 players

2 players

3 players

4 players

5 players

4 players

2 players

3 players

4 players

3 players

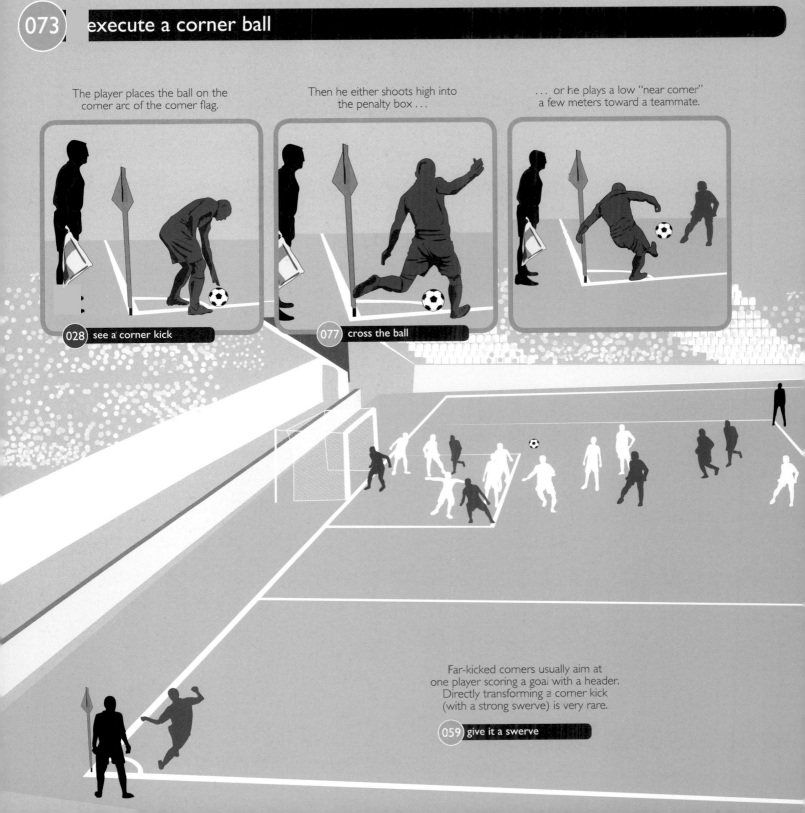

execute a corner ball

The player places the ball on the corner arc of the corner flag.

Then he either shoots high into the penalty box . . .

. . . or he plays a low "near corner" a few meters toward a teammate.

(028) see a corner kick

(077) cross the ball

Far-kicked corners usually aim at one player scoring a goal with a header. Directly transforming a corner kick (with a strong swerve) is very rare.

(059) give it a swerve

throw it in

026 watch a throw-in

The player must throw with both hands behind his head.

Running up is allowed. But the player's face needs to be directed at the playing field ...

... and parts of both feet need to be touching the ground during the throw.

Passing means to play the ball to another teammate. There are low passes, high passes, quick, long, short, and misdirected passes.

You play a pass during build-up to gain space (or time) and to assist shots on goal. Makes sense, doesn't it?

Passing the ball through the legs of an opponent is called "nutmegging"—an irritating move.

055 use your heel

Passing with the heel can look elegant, or arrogant, depending on the perspective.

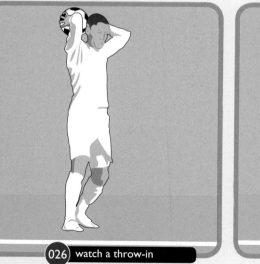

perform long passes

A long pass into the free area is also called deep pass or deep forward pass. The player needs to calculate or anticipate his teammate's path well.

cross the ball

Playing a high ball, e.g., from the sidelines into the opponent's penalty box, is called crossing.

understand one-twos

Direct passes between players using the space past the opponent are called one-twos!

understand misdirected passes

A pass that lands in front of the opponent's feet instead of the teammate's is called a misdirected pass, or simply: bad pass.

The player stands with his back to the goal, lunges out with one leg and kicks the flying ball with the other while falling backwards. This difficult kicking technique is named after the Italian soccer player Silvio Piola.

The player spins on his own axis while running and takes the ball past the opponent—first with one sole, then with the other. The French player Zinédine Zidane was a master of this complicated trick.

The Brazilian soccer player Ronaldinho kicks the
ball over his head and stops it with the back
of his neck to pop it back forwards and
take it with him while running.

While running, the ball is quickly kicked
past the standing leg from behind to mislead the
opponent. This move is named after
Johan Cruyff, a Dutch soccer star.

Wedged between heel and instep, the ball is kicked from behind over one's head to the front. This trick was the speciality of the Nigerian soccer player Jay-Jay Okocha.

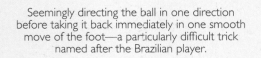

Seemingly directing the ball in one direction
before taking it back immediately in one smooth
move of the foot—a particularly difficult trick
named after the Brazilian player.

The Kuntz saw

Thank the Lord!

I don't cheer for goals against my team.

The mask

The pacifier

The Miro Klose

The flic-flac

The heart

The Cristiano Ronaldo

The kiss

The knee slide

The cradle

Kissing the wedding ring

The diver

The flip

The glider

learn the line-up

Each player has a position and a task. Together with the tactics the line-up creates the plan of the game.

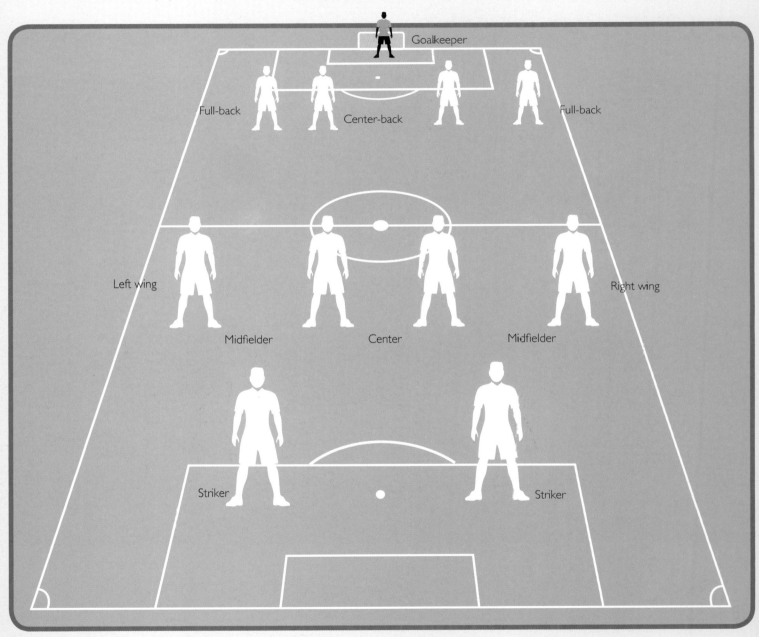

Line-ups are indicated with three or four digits (e.g. 4-4-2 or 4-3-2-1). The numbers represent full-back–midfielder–striker.
Four-digit rows have modern positions like "defensive midfielder."

Originally forward passes were not allowed, which is why the players moved in a row across the field.

pick up the 2-3-5 pyramid formation

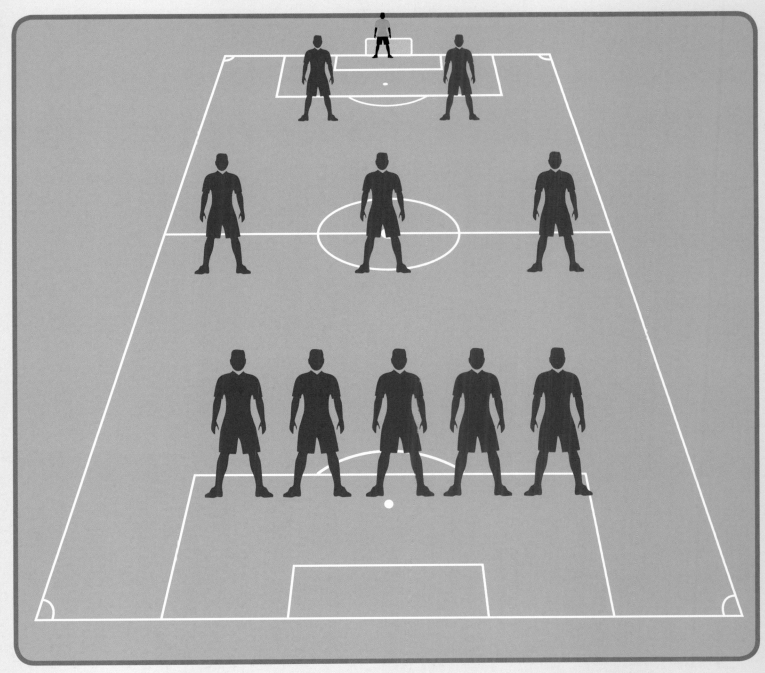

This was one of the very first formations. The shirt numbers 1–11 were assigned from the back to the front.

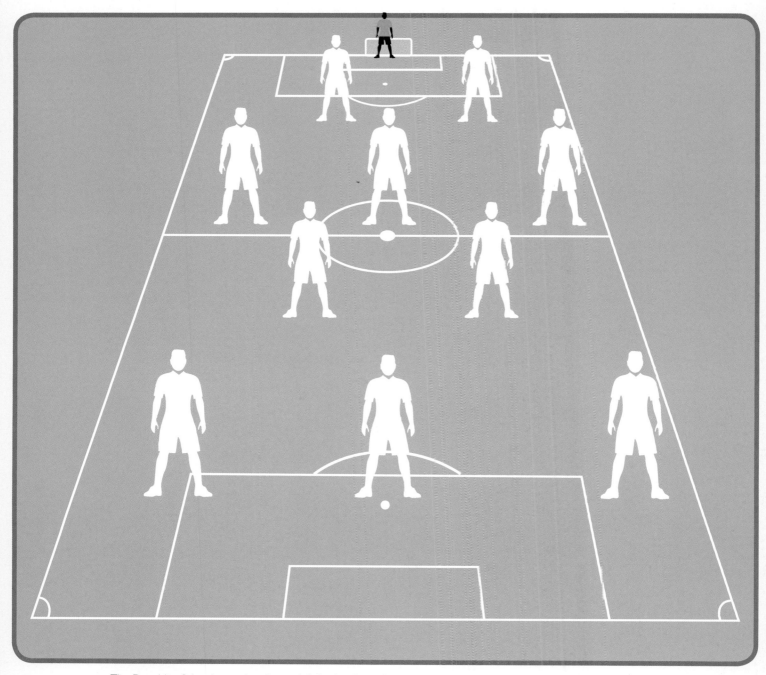

The Danubian School was played especially in the Czech Republic, Austria, and Hungary, and adopted by the Italians.

This formation is offense-oriented and is associated with Dutch soccer as well as with FC Barcelona.

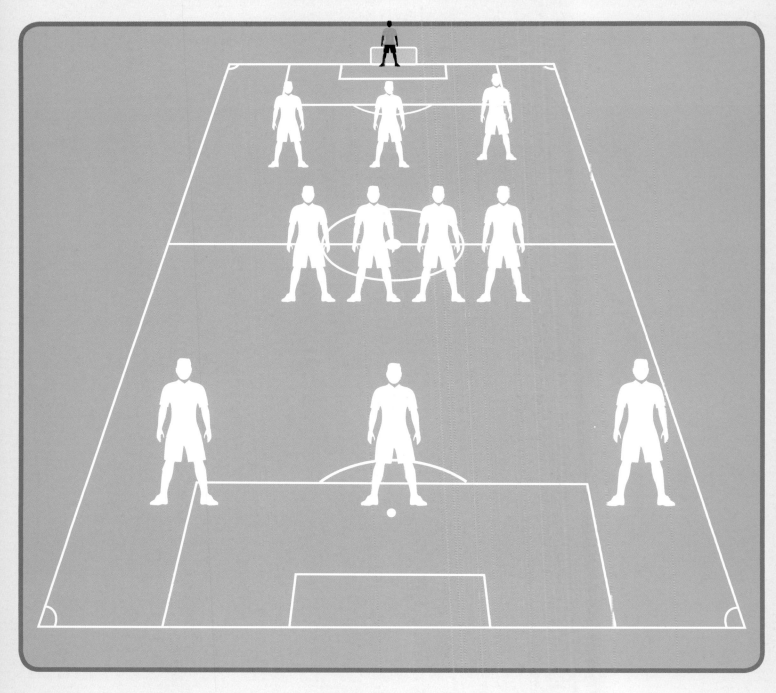

This formation is typically played when the team needs to catch up.

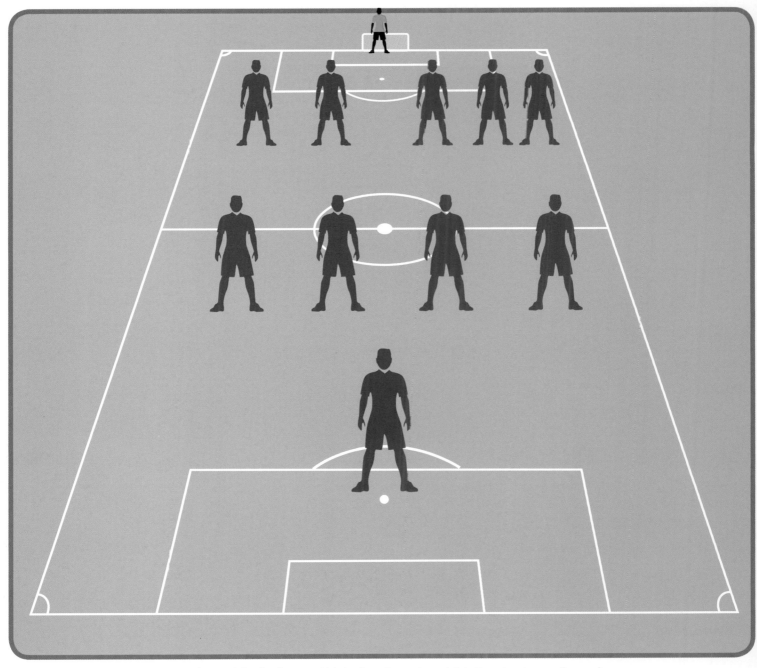

A very defensive line-up which is often chosen to maintain the advantage or the result.

This formation was introduced by Guardiola to FC Bayern in 2013. Spain had become European champion with it in 2008.

Game with a libero (last man in front of the goalkeeper).

Both France and Italy played in this formation at the 2006 World Cup final.

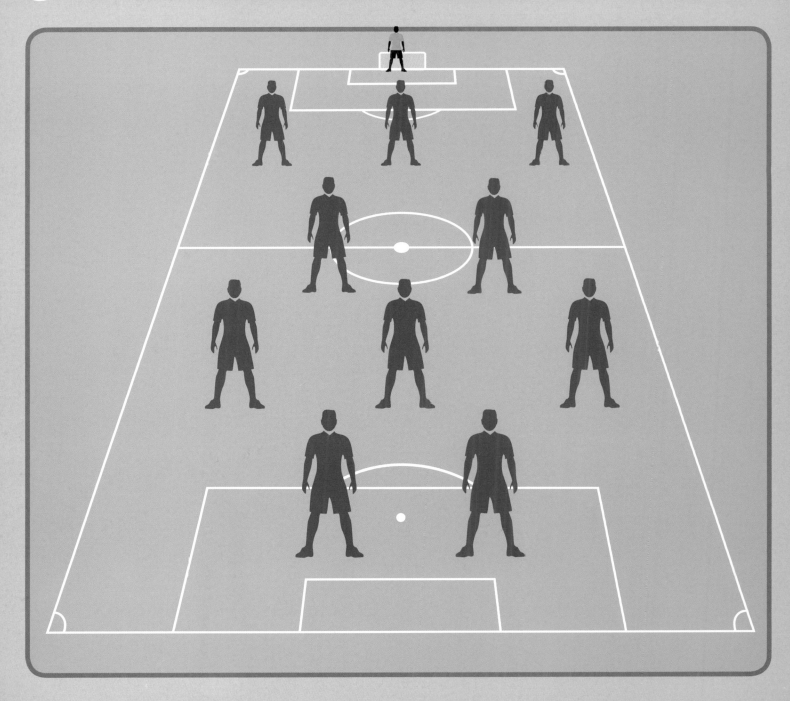

Inter Milan played this defensive formation very successfully in the 1960s. It was developed by the Austrian Karl Rappan in the 1930s.

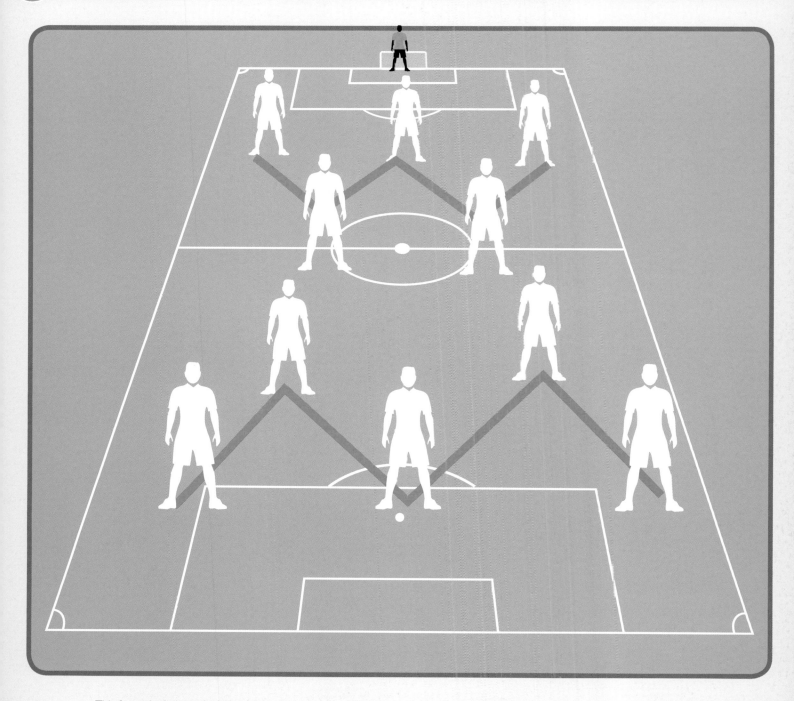

This formation's name is derived from the position of the players. It was developed by Herbert Chapman, the trainer of Arsenal.

This formation was especially popular in the 1990s. The English soccer magazine FourFourTwo is named after it.

The formation 4-3-1-2 depicted above is a modern variation of the traditional 4-3-3.

Offense

Defense

Through man-to-man marking, players are each assigned to fixed opponents, whose actions they need to obstruct during a match.

Offense

Defense

During zone defense the players' positions shift with the ball. Zone defense demands constant observation of the whole game. Switching from defense to offense is easier here.

The player shields the ball by turning his body and stays in ball possession.

Pressing means to disrupt the ball-carrying opponent early on within one's own half and to prevent the build-up.

This way you force the opponent to make mistakes, and have good prospects of possessing the ball.

The defender in white takes the ball off the blue scorer and passes it on quickly with a counter.

To counter means to quickly switch from defense to counterattack. Here the defense needs to rethink fast and initiate attacks and the scorers need to be able to free themselves cleverly.

As few passes as possible ought to be played during a counter. Ideally only deep passes are played in order to reach the goal of the opponent quickly and in ambush-style.

During an offense through the middle the spaces are often narrow. You need to dismantle the opponent's defense move after move and then reach the goal with short and quick passes (short passing game). Technically versed midfielders are needed for this.

Offense along the wings calls for wingers who are vocal and strong in dribbling as well as center-forwards who are good at headers. Here you try to outsmart the left and right defenders and play the ball to the center of the penalty box from the sides.

Minimum age of 12

Member of a soccer club

20—50 h

20—50 hours training

20X

Lead at least 20 games per year

A referee should also be physically fit and
ready to take part in eight to twelve
advanced training events per year.

Physical fitness

038 understand a warning / yellow card

Booking: yellow card

039 understand a sending-off / red card

Dismissal: red card

024 watch the kickoff

Start of the game

027 get a goal kick

The goalkeeper kicks the ball into the field

Safe sign: the game continues and is not interrupted.

043 understand substitution

Player substitution or the ball was not played from a resting position during a free kick.

028 see a corner kick

Corner kick

031 see an indirect free kick

Indirect free kick

030 see a direct free kick

Direct free kick

033 witness a penalty kick

Penalty kick

032 determine an advantage

Advantage

Final whistle

034   see offsides

Offside

034   see offsides

Offside position at the opposite side
of the playing field

034   see offsides

Offside position near the linesman

034   see offsides

Offside position in the middle
of the playing field

026   watch a throw-in

Throw-in

043 understand substitution

Substitution

062 understand fouls

Foul by a defender

Shows the half time progression

062 understand fouls

Foul by an offender

watch the game

A

Away supporters: fan curve of the rivaling team's supporters

B

Banana shot: a ball with a curving trajectory

Battle cry: the chants of a team's fans

Block tackle: a ball that is kicked simultaneously by two players (can hurt but is not considered a foul)

Box: penalty box

C

Catenaccio: typical Italian defensive work

Caretaker manager: a trainer who manages a team temporarily

Consolation goal: the first goal of the losing team without the prospect of an equalizer

Corner of the goal post: the upper corner of the goal

Crossbar: upper margin of the goal

Cross pass: a pass between two players who are on the same level

D

Deflecting: averting the ball by the goalkeeper

E

Extra time: additional playing time when the score is tied

F

Far corner: a ball that is kicked in the direction of the far post

G

Goalhanger: a scorer who builds on the other players' work and scores a more or less easy goal

Golden goal: the goal that decides which team wins the match

H

Handball: ball played with the hand, e.g. by the goalkeeper

Heat battle: term for a game played at more than 77°F / 25°C—famous example: the heat battle of Lausanne, Austria-Switzerland (World Cup 1954) at 104°F / 40°C in the shade.

Hooligans: overzealous sports fans who engage in violence or vandalism

I

International cap: international soccer match

J

Joker: a player, usually a striker, who is brought in to turn the game around or to bring about a decision

K

Kop: short for Spion Kop; describes a number of terraces and stands in stadiums attended by hardcore fans which resembles Spion Kop Hill in South Africa

L

Last sixteen: the last sixteen teams left in a tournament, also known as pre-quarter finals

Left-back: full-back defenders on the left side

Lob: an expressively lifted ball that outplays the opponent or goalkeeper

Lucky shot: a successful shot on goal based on luck

M

Making a stand: to make it clear to the rival team through a rough foul that there's nothing to be gained—e.g. ,right after kickoff at top games

N

No-Look pass: a pass wherein the player doesn't look in the direction he passes the ball

Nutmegging: to play the ball through the legs of a rival goalkeeper or player

O

Overtime: additional playing time when the score is tied (also called extra time)

P

Penalty shootout: to perform a penalty kick

Penalty: a penalty kick

Pencil jump: a ball that jumps straight up

Professional foul: a deliberate foul of the opponent to avert a goal

Punching away: the goalkeeper averts the ball with his fists

Pussyfooting: a game situation where nothing happens—if this lasts for more than ten minutes, the game is considered disjointed

Q

Quarter final: last eight competitors left in a tournament

R

Rabona: a particularly elaborate shot where the free leg kicks behind the standing leg

S

Second yellow card: receiving a red card after having previously received a yellow card

Silverware: cup/trophy won in a match

Single-elimination tournament: competition wherein each loser is immediately eliminated after a match

Sweeper: a player who blocks the center-forward of the other team in the 4-3-3 formation

Swirling ball: a ball conceived for the 2010 World Cup ("Jabulani," which seems to have a life of its own; when shot hard it "swirls," usually past the perplexed goalkeeper)

T

Technical area: a marked-off area outside of the playing field where doctors and stand-by players are located

Tifosi: Italian fans

Tiki-taka: a perfect short passing game over several stages

U

Ultras: song-crazy fan group, provides permanent support

V

Veteran player: a player who can't be fooled, has an incredible amount of experience, seems immune to injuries and set-backs, and is still a secret weapon even in advanced years

W

Water battle: a game that takes place during/after a downpour—famous example: the water battle of Frankfurt, Germany-Poland (World Cup 1974)

X

X: marking an anticipated tie between teams on a betting pools coupon

Y

Youngster: a young and talented player

Z

Zizou: nickname for the famous French soccer player Zinedine Zidane

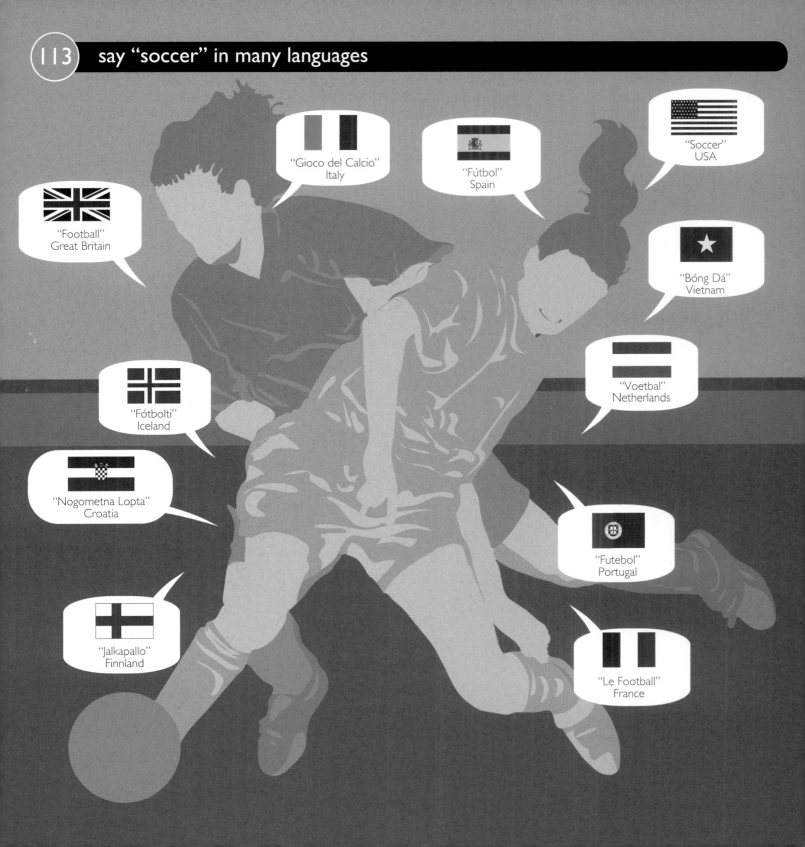

Mega events raise the sales for breweries.

15 million balls from the 2006 World Cup are said to have been sold. World Cup team shirts were also sold by the millions.

Panini Germany made record sales proceeds of 85 million euro by selling stickers—roughly 30 million more than in the following non-World Cup year.

120 take a look at fan gear

China profits from the production of various merchandise articles—flags, shirts, caps, and vuvuzelas—as well as from the production of merchandise imitations.

207 find the tv cameras

Broadcasting World Cup games leads to high ratings for television networks.

135 get the right tv

Sales of TV sets soar one week before the first kickoff of a World Cup.

Both FIFA (World Cup) and UEFA (European Championship) or rather, their respective continental associations, profit from higher revenues.

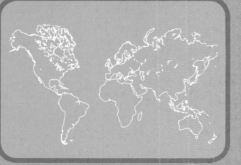

Host countries of mega events profit from considerable investment effects and a surplus in hotel bookings.

The agents (players and trainers) ultimately profit from an increased market value and higher salaries.

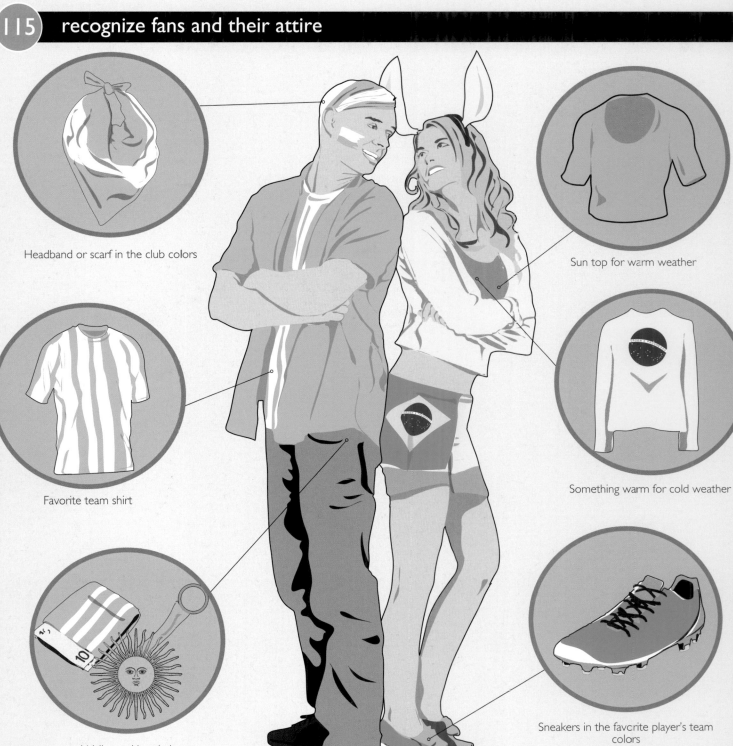

Headband or scarf in the club colors

Sun top for warm weather

Favorite team shirt

Something warm for cold weather

Wallet and keychain

Sneakers in the favorite player's team colors

Christmas tree balls of the favorite team for diehard fans—St. Pauli Christmas tree balls are iconic!

The club's emblem or toast

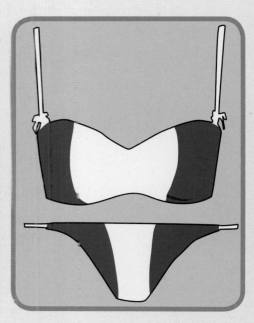

Club colors right on the skin—e.g., with a bikini in club or national colors

Some fans go nuts (for waffles)

Soccer rubber duck

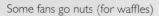

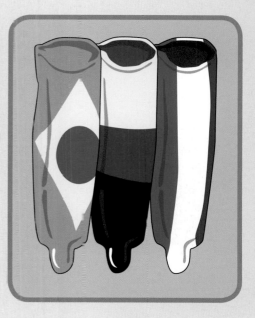

Some games last longer than 90 minutes…

117 see which sports divisions have the most stadium spectators

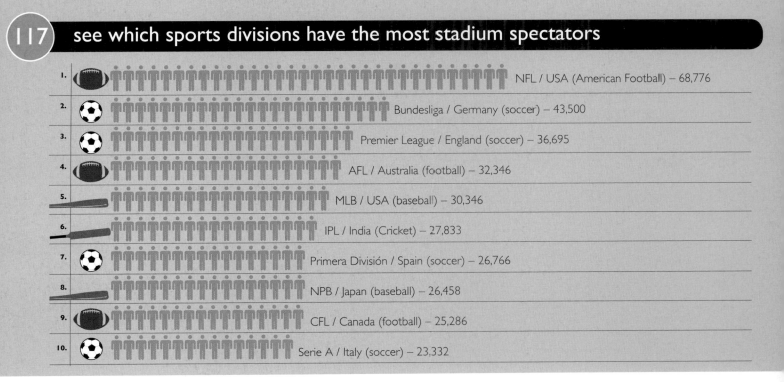

1. NFL / USA (American Football) – 68,776
2. Bundesliga / Germany (soccer) – 43,500
3. Premier League / England (soccer) – 36,695
4. AFL / Australia (football) – 32,346
5. MLB / USA (baseball) – 30,346
6. IPL / India (Cricket) – 27,833
7. Primera División / Spain (soccer) – 26,766
8. NPB / Japan (baseball) – 26,458
9. CFL / Canada (football) – 25,286
10. Serie A / Italy (soccer) – 23,332

118 count the clubs with the most stadium spectators

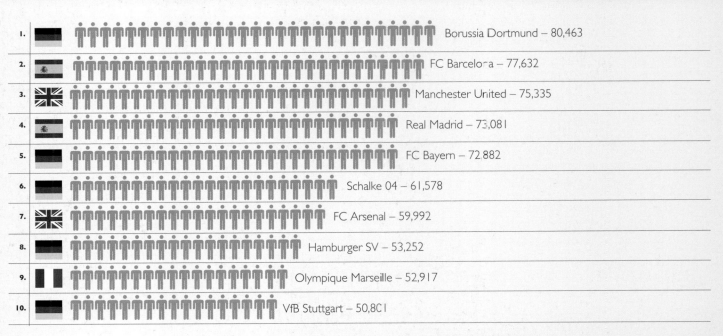

1. Borussia Dortmund – 80,463
2. FC Barcelona – 77,632
3. Manchester United – 75,335
4. Real Madrid – 73,081
5. FC Bayern – 72,882
6. Schalke 04 – 61,578
7. FC Arsenal – 59,992
8. Hamburger SV – 53,252
9. Olympique Marseille – 52,917
10. VfB Stuttgart – 50,801

The numbers in the two statistics are average values of the years 2013–2015.

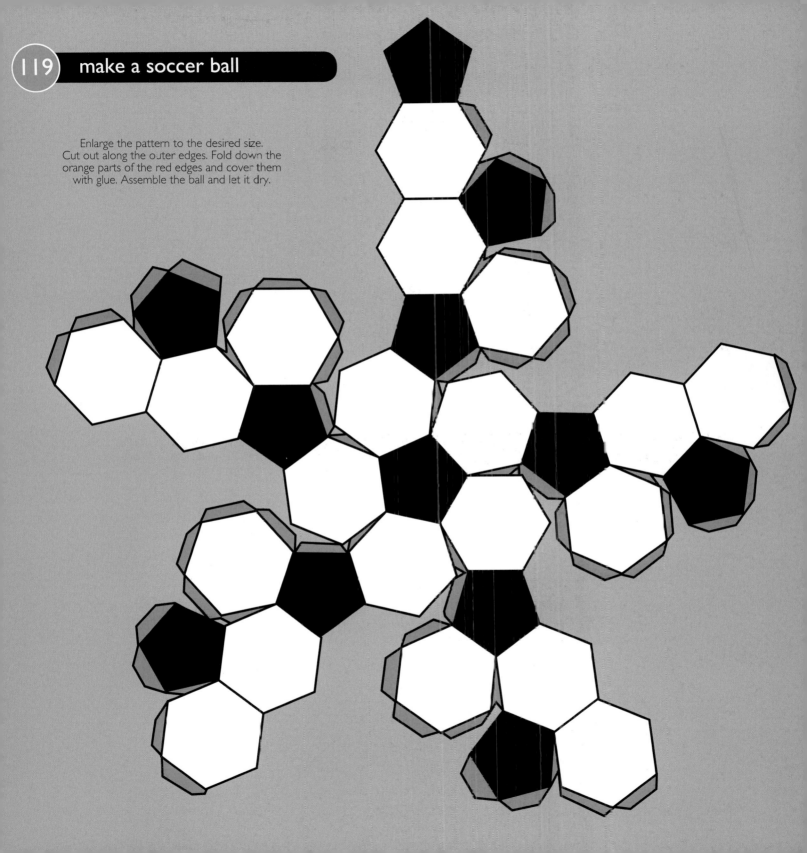

make a soccer ball

Enlarge the pattern to the desired size.
Cut out along the outer edges. Fold down the
orange parts of the red edges and cover them
with glue. Assemble the ball and let it dry.

Inflatable fan hand

Soccer bunny ears

Standard equipment: the fan scarf

Fan hat in team colors

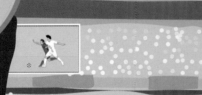

Wooden clacker to make some noise

Vuvuzela; forbidden in some places due to their dangerous effects on hearing (127 decibels)!

Other fan accessories (here: a Hawaiian lei)

Drums—a rhythm machine for fan chants

One flag is nice—but many flags make for a sea!

Use make-up sticks. Draw a black rectangle and divide it into three sections.

Color the first section blue.

Color the second section white, the third section red.

Vive la France!

Pull back hair. Apply make-up color with a sponge.

Avoid eye area. Spread color up to the hairline.

Finish off the eye area with a brush.

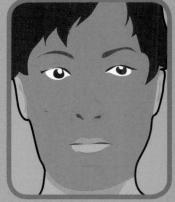

Line the upper eyelid with black khol.

Apply black eyeshadow on the brow ridge.

Spread red eyeshadow across the upper eyelid.

Apply yellow eyeshadow above the lashes.

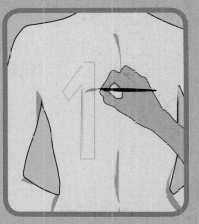

Use bodypaint color. Start by outlining the numbers.

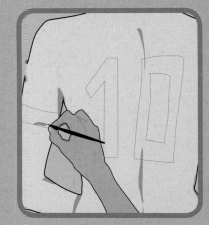

Draw the outlines of the jersey.

Color in the numbers.

Fill in the main color.

Add shading and detail.

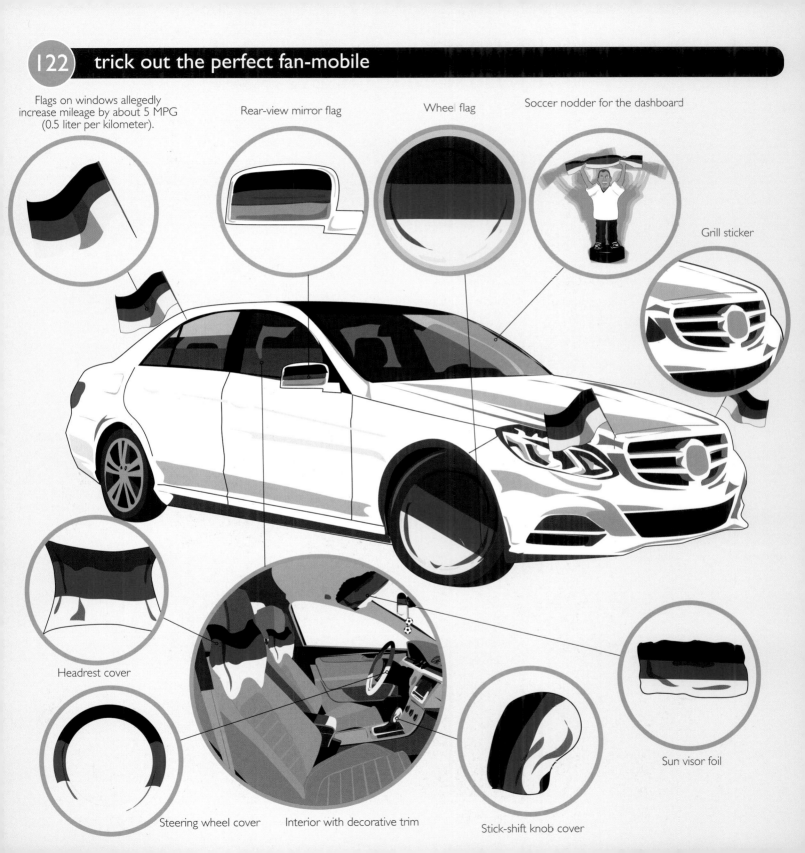

Flags on windows allegedly increase mileage by about 5 MPG (0.5 liter per kilometer).

Rear-view mirror flag

Wheel flag

Soccer nodder for the dashboard

Grill sticker

Headrest cover

Steering wheel cover

Interior with decorative trim

Stick-shift knob cover

Sun visor foil

Choose national colors.
Cut into straws vertically.

Attach straws to spokes.

Secure with tape.

Tie three short scarves
around the seatpost.
(Don't let them reach
to the spokes.)

Measure and cut adhesive foil.

Fit exactly and smooth down.

Press down edges.

Now, you've got yourself
a "national pole".

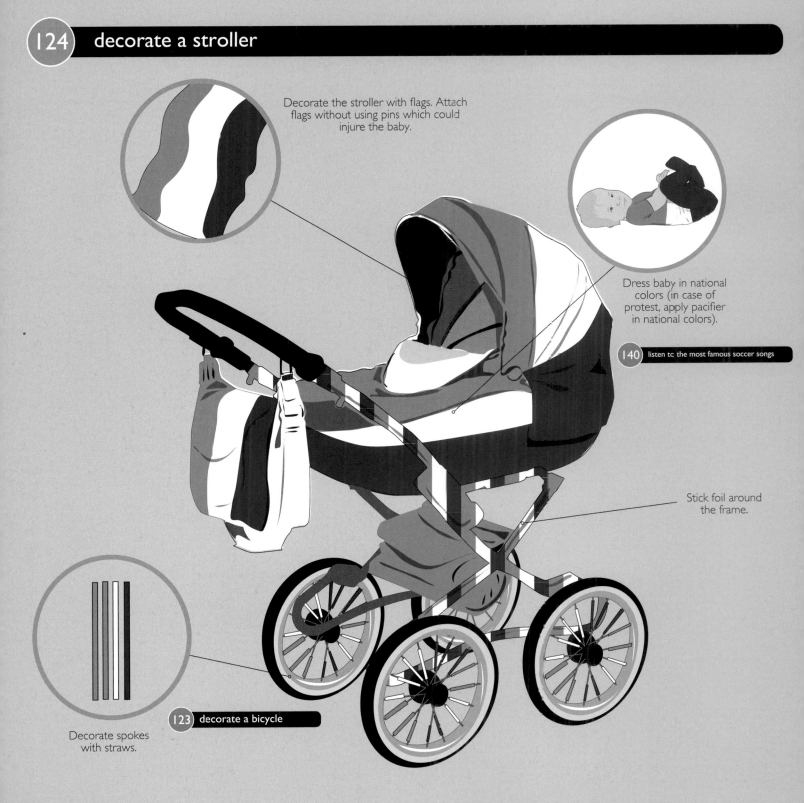

Decorate the stroller with flags. Attach flags without using pins which could injure the baby.

Dress baby in national colors (in case of protest, apply pacifier in national colors).

140 listen to the most famous soccer songs

Stick foil around the frame.

123 decorate a bicycle

Decorate spokes with straws.

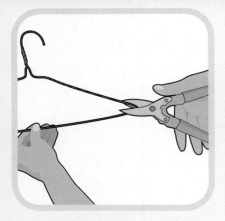

Cut off the horizontal wires of
three metal coathangers.

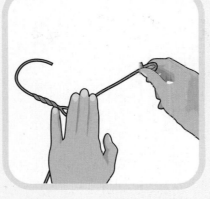

Bend wire ends to form eyelets.

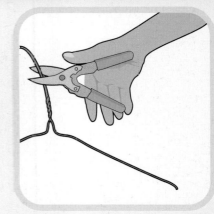

Shorten hooks of two hangers.

Wrap tape around it.

Arrange the three wires.

Secure with tape.

Draw hexagons on little styrofoam balls.

Color in black fields and attach balls
to the metal eyelets.

Hang out of reach of the baby.

126 carve a potato stamp

Halve a potato.

Sketch pattern.

Cut out background.

Dip stamp in color.

Goal!

127 fill a soccer snow globe

Use a clean jar with a screw-on lid.

Hard boil an egg and chop up the eggshell.

Mix water and glycerin 1:1 and pour into the jar.

Glue figure onto the inside of the lid.

Screw lid on tight. Shake.

128 dye a t-shirt in national colors

Gather the middle.

Twist.

Secure with yarn.

Apply fabric color and let it absorb.

Rinse and wear.

The Netherlands fan

The France fan

The Germany fan

The Italy fan

Special clubs offer Christmas tree ornaments in club colors.

Pick a comfortable couch.

135 get the right TV

Place TV optimally.

Join in singing the national anthems.

Place beer bottles and opener within reach.

133 try out the favorite soccer fan snacks

Provide snacks.

Pizza in national or club colors (e.g., Italian topping with tomatoes, mozzarella, and spinach).

Follow Liveticker.

In case of goals cheer as much as your circulatory system allows.

Smug remarks: Yes! Violence: No!

Meet with friends for a public viewing. Wear comfortable clothes and provide fan gear. Public viewing has become particularly popular in Germany since the 2006 Word Cup.

120 take a look at fan gear

115 recognize fans and their attire

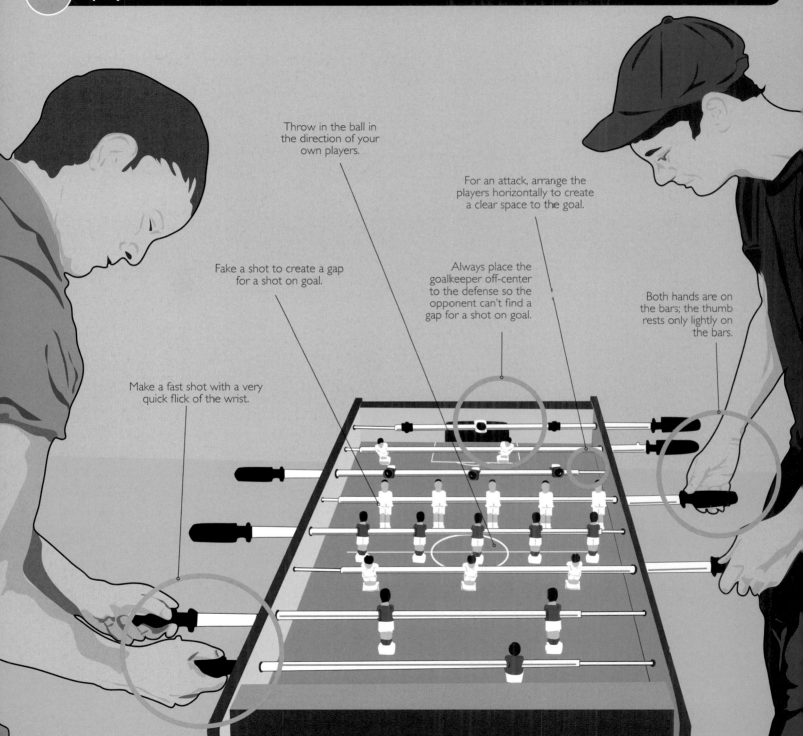

Throw in the ball in the direction of your own players.

For an attack, arrange the players horizontally to create a clear space to the goal.

Fake a shot to create a gap for a shot on goal.

Always place the goalkeeper off-center to the defense so the opponent can't find a gap for a shot on goal.

Both hands are on the bars; the thumb rests only lightly on the bars.

Make a fast shot with a very quick flick of the wrist.

Sunflower seeds are very popular in Russia.

Galette saucisse are the French version of hot dogs.

Simit, sesame rings, are the Turks' favorite stadium snack.

French fries with mayonnaise are the Belgian national dish—also in the stadium!

Chin chin, fried dough bits from Nigeria, are popular throughout Africa.

Ćevapi are eaten particularly in Bosnia and Herzegovina in the stadium.

Biltong, a type of beef jerky, is eaten in Africa and also in America.

Soccer fans in Spain and Latin America eat filled pastries known as empanadas.

Canadian fans love poutine: French fries with cheese and gravy.

Souvlaki is eaten in Greek stadiums.

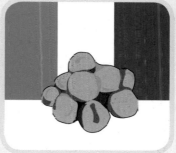
Arancini, fried rice balls with filling, are the Italian stadium snack.

It's hard to imagine a German stadium without currywurst, and it is also popular worldwide.

Ketchup

Hot grill sauce

Bratwursts

Burgers

Hot dogs

Mustard

Potato salad

Chicken wings

Currywurst

Cut into edge crosswise.

Marinate and let cool for six hours.

Place on the preheated grill.

Flip and turn to create a grill pattern.

Check temperature: 22°F / 50°C bloody; 158°F / 70°C done.

French fries

Sufficient beer supply

Rub with butter and spices.

Open beer can and remove lid.

Pour in spices

Sit chicken on top of the beer can

Grill for about 90 minutes.

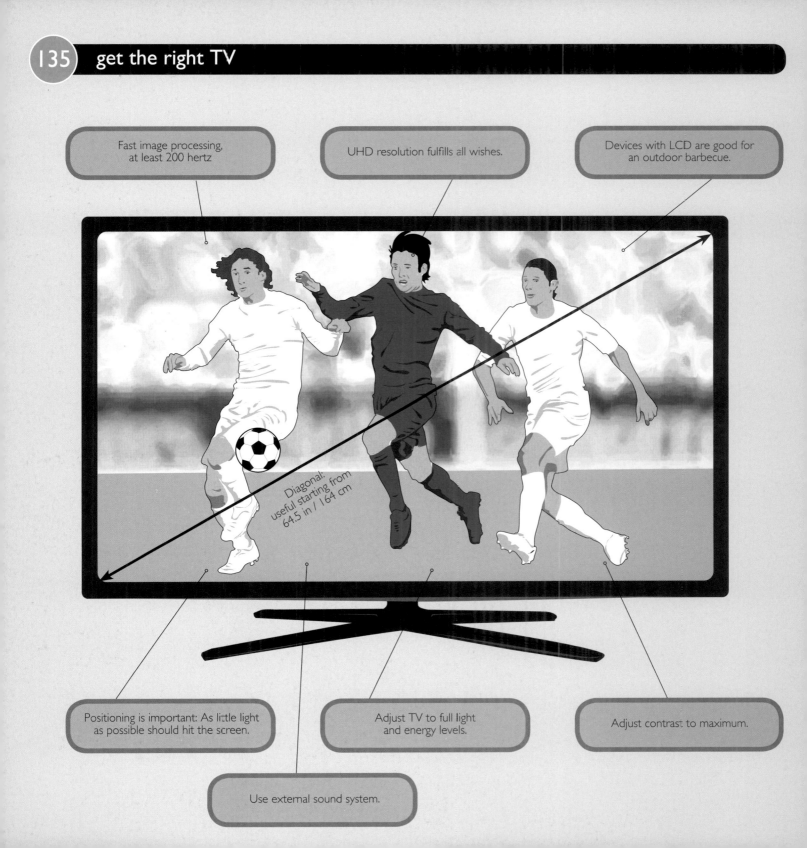

Fast image processing, at least 200 hertz

UHD resolution fulfills all wishes.

Devices with LCD are good for an outdoor barbecue.

Diagonal: useful starting from 64.5 in / 164 cm

Positioning is important: As little light as possible should hit the screen.

Adjust TV to full light and energy levels.

Adjust contrast to maximum.

Use external sound system.

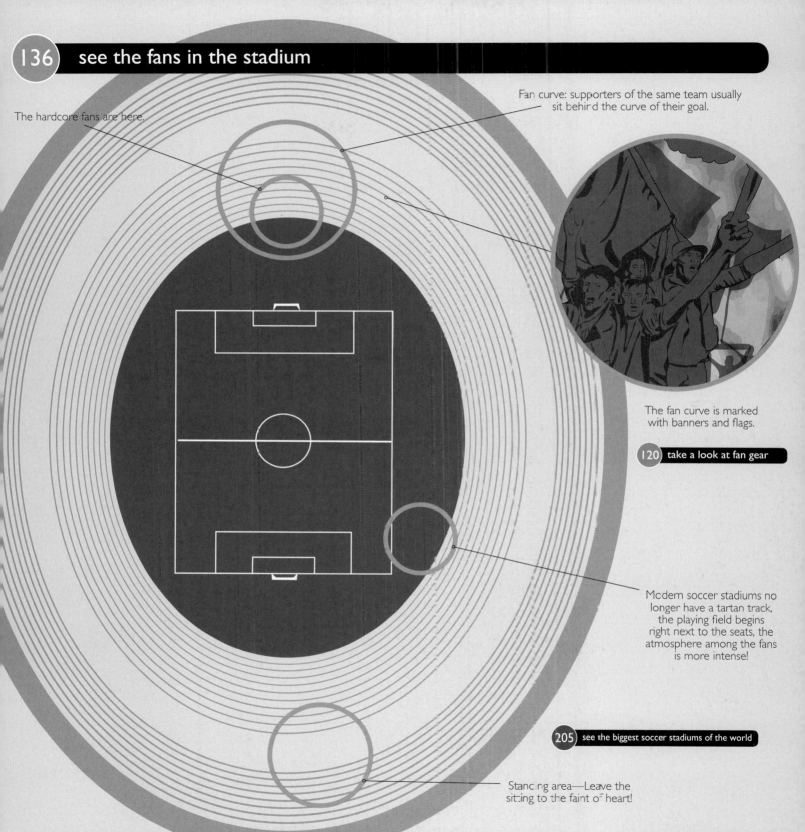

The hardcore fans are here.

Fan curve: supporters of the same team usually sit behind the curve of their goal.

The fan curve is marked with banners and flags.

120 take a look at fan gear

Modern soccer stadiums no longer have a tartan track, the playing field begins right next to the seats, the atmosphere among the fans is more intense!

205 see the biggest soccer stadiums of the world

Standing area—Leave the sitting to the faint of heart!

A hooligan is a fan of a soccer team who is ready to use violence.

Hooligans of Atlético Nacional (Columbia)
Drug lord Pablo Escobar financed the team in the 1980s. In 2012, a man was shot in the head and killed and 315 people were arrested during a veritable battle with fans of Independiente Medellín.

Hooligans of Catania (Italy)
In 2007, a policeman was killed at a match against Palermo.

Hooligans of the Newell's Old Boys (Argentina)
In 2010, a 14-year-old and a hooligan mentor were shot.

Hooligans of Wisla Krakau (Polen)
In 2011, twelve hooligans armed with machetes and baseball bats killed a rival fan.

Hooligans of Galatasaray Istanbul (Turkey)
"Welcome to hell"—that is how violent hooligans of Galatasaray greet rival fans in Istanbul.

Hooligans of the Corinthians Paulista (Brazil)
Brazilian hooligans—who want to fight in the first row—need to master a combat sport like Muay Thai or jiujitsu (that is what the group demands). Only the top third comes into bodily contact with the enemy. Behind them their supporters, the "oba oba," spur their fighters on.

Hooligans of Al-Masry (Egypt)
During a derby in Cairo, the hooligans caused a mass panic. 74 people were killed and 248 more were injured.

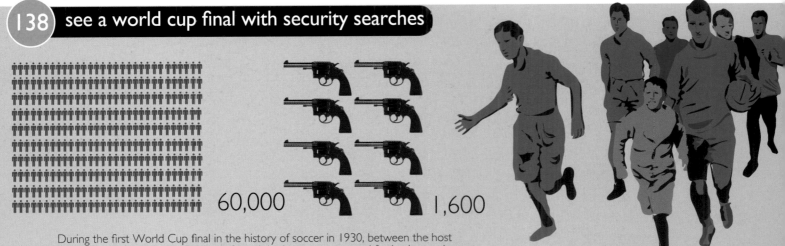

60,000   1,600

During the first World Cup final in the history of soccer in 1930, between the host Uruguay and Argentina, the Belgian referee John Langenus arranged for body searches of the more than 60,000 spectators before kickoff. More than 1,600 revolvers were collected.

The wave always moves clockwise. It moves up to 20–25 seats per second through the stadium (roughly 36–39 ft / 11–12 m per second). The wave oscillates between 16–36 feet / 5–11 m.

**Gerry & The Pacemakers
"You'll Never Walk
Alone" (1963)**
Liverpool FC's "Kop"
made this probably
the most famous soccer
song worldwide.

**Lightning Seeds
"Three Lions" (1996)**
The official hymn of the
English national soccer
team for the European
Championship in 1996
on home turf.

**The White Stripes
"Seven Nation Army"
(2003)**
This song was played at the
European Championship
in 2008 when the teams
entered the field. The
Italians even adopted the
song for their national
team's unofficial hymn.

**Queen
"We Are The Champions"
(1977)**
Whenever something outstanding
happens this song is played.
The hit became the official World
Cup song in 1994; Crazy Frog
recorded a version of the song
for the 2006 World Cup.

Blur – "Song 2" (1997)
Goal hymn of clubs like
OSC Lille and FC St. Pauli.

**Shakira
"Waka Waka (This Time
For Africa)" (2010)**
The Columbian singer Shakira
chose an African chorus for her
World Cup song based on the
chorus of the song "Zangaléwa"
by the Cameroonian band Golden
Sounds. "Waka Waka" is thus an
African variant of "Come on!"

**Die Toten Hosen
"Bayern" (2000)**
With their anti-Bayern
hymn, the Fortuna
Düsseldorf supporters
sang their way into the
hearts of many soccer-
crazy Germans.

**Ricky Martin
"La Copa De La Vida
(Cup Of Life)" (1998)**
"Allez, allez, allez"—the
text of the chorus already
indicates that this is the
official song of the 1998
World Cup in France.

hear the official fifa world cup hymns and songs

Since 1962, the FIFA has chosen the official World Cup hymn or official World Cup song. Anyone can take part in the SuperSong contest; 1,500 songs from all over the world were submitted for the 2014 World Cup alone. The songs are performed by an international celebrity.

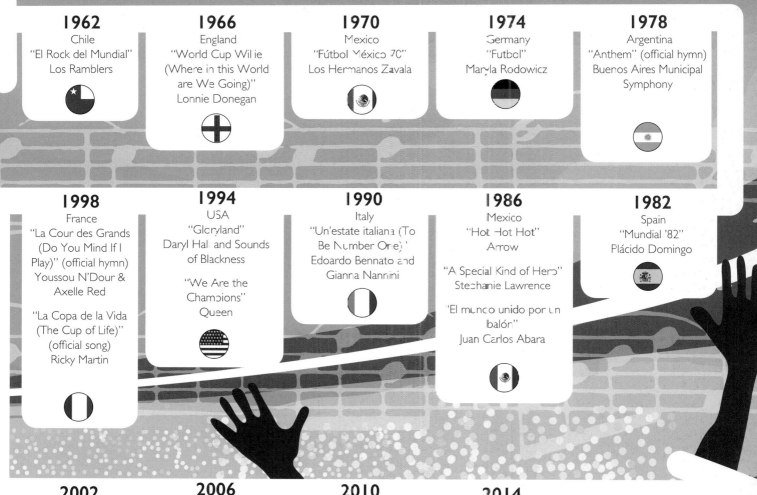

1962
Chile
"El Rock del Mundial"
Los Ramblers

1966
England
"World Cup Willie
(Where in this World
are We Going)"
Lonnie Donegan

1970
Mexico
"Fútbol México 70"
Los Hermanos Zavala

1974
Germany
"Futbol"
Maryla Rodowicz

1978
Argentina
"Anthem" (official hymn)
Buenos Aires Municipal
Symphony

1998
France
"La Cour des Grands
(Do You Mind If I
Play)" (official hymn)
Youssou N'Dour &
Axelle Red

"La Copa de la Vida
(The Cup of Life)"
(official song)
Ricky Martin

1994
USA
"Gloryland"
Daryl Hall and Sounds
of Blackness

"We Are the
Champions"
Queen

1990
Italy
"Un'estate italiana (To
Be Number One)"
Edoardo Bennato and
Gianna Nannini

1986
Mexico
"Hot Hot Hot"
Arrow

"A Special Kind of Hero"
Stephanie Lawrence

"El mundo unido por un
balón"
Juan Carlos Abara

1982
Spain
"Mundial '82"
Plácido Domingo

2002
South Korea
Japan
(Jointly Hosted)
"Anthem"
(official hymn)
Vangelis

"Boom"
(official song)
Anastacia

2006
Germany
"Zeit dass sich was dreht
(Celebrate The Day)"
(official hymn)
Grönemeyer featuring
Amadou & Mariam

"The Time of Our Lives"
(official song)
Il Divo featuring Toni
Braxton

2010
South Africa
"Sign of a Victory"
(official hymn)
R. Kelly featuring Soweto
Spiritual Singers

"Waka Waka"
(official song)
Shakira featuring
Freshlyground

2014
Brazil
"Dar um Jeito
(We Will Find a Way)"
(official hymn)
Carlos Santana featuring
Wyclef & Avicii &
Alexandre Pires

"We Are One
(Ole Ola)" (official song)
Pitbull featuring Jennifer
Lopez & Claudia Leitte

Pinball

Jürgen Klinsmann (Germany): Was given the nickname "pinball" because the ball often bounced away from him.

Llama

Frank Rijkaard (Netherlands): During the last sixteen rounds of the 1990 World Cup, he spat in the direction of Rudi Völler. For millions this made him "the llama" from then on.

Non-flying Dutchman

Dennis Bergkamp (Netherlands): Due to his severe fear of flying he was called "the non-flying Dutchman."

Ball lightning

Ailton Gonçalves da Silva, short Ailton (Brazil): He was called "ball lightning" because of his explosive acceleration.

Heintje

Andreas Möller (Germany): Was known in the soccer world as the player who "wept easily," which is why he was given the nickname Heintje, named after the young Dutch singer with the hit "Mama."

Tante Käthe

Rudi Völler (Germany): His bubble perm is to blame for his nickname Tante Käthe (aunt Kate).

Titan

Oliver Kahn (Germany): His impassibility in the goal during the 2002 World Cup earned him the name of "titan."

La pulga

Lionel Messi (Argentina): Not particularly tall—which is why he is called "la pulga," the flea.

Kaiser

Franz Beckenbauer (Germany): Beckenbauer let himself be photographed next to Emperor (Kaiser) Franz Joseph I of Austria—he was called "Fußballkaiser" (soccer emperor) in a soccer magazine; the name "Kaiser" stuck.

Goleador

Hans Krankl (Austria): He played for FC Barcelona and became the Spanish top scorer for the Catalans in his first season with 29 championship goals, which earned him the nickname of "goleador."

The paper-thin

Matthias Sindelar (Austria): Due to his delicate form he was called "der Papierene," the "paper-thin."

Black panther

Eusébio (Portugal), an Africa-born player, was known as "the black panther" in the media for his speed.

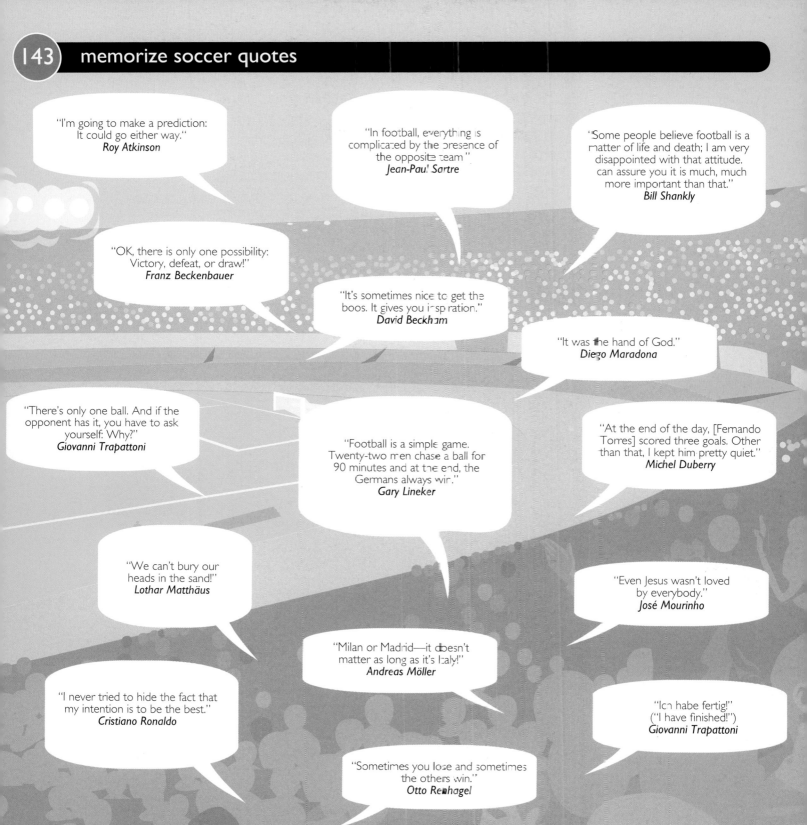

Copy the picture—enlarge if needed—and color it in!

know the facts

2000 BCE

Cuju ("cu" = kick with the foot, "ju" = ball) is played in China.

500 CE

According to legend, people in China play with an air-filled ball for the first time. In ancient Greece and Rome, ball games are played for military and bodily exercise.

11th century

In early medieval England, the gates of towns and villages serve as the goal for the kickers and the space between the localities as the "field."

12th century

In France, women and men play *la sioule*, a precursor to modern soccer.

1839

Charles Goodyear develops a rubber ball; 24 years later H.J. Lindon creates an inflatable rubber bladder for soccer balls that can be inflated with a pump.

1846

Students of the University of Cambridge make a first rough draft of rules.

1857

Founding of the first official soccer club in England: Sheffield F.C.

1863

Founding of the first FA (football association).

1872

Designation of a homogenous ball size; First international cap between Scotland and England (0-0).

1878

First soccer match lit by electric lighting.

1879

Founding of the FC St. Gallen (oldest existing soccer club in Switzerland).

1882

Founding of the IFAB (International Football Association Board) in London.

1894

Founding of the first women's soccer team, calling itself the British Ladies.

1900

Founding of the German soccer association; soccer is made an Olympic event.

1902

First international cap on the European continent: Austria versus Hungary (5-0).

1904

The FIFA is founded in Paris.

1914–1918

Founding of the French women's sports association (Fédération des Sociétés Féminines Sportives de France).

1921

Stadium ban for women in England.

1930

Organization of the first World Cup through the FIFA; Founding of the first women's club, the "Damen-Fussball-Club" (ladies' soccer club) in Frankfurt

1939

Official introduction of shirt numbers.

1949

Removeable studs for boots are used for the first time.

1954

Founding of the UEFA in Basel.

1971

First women's association champion in Germany.

1991

First women's soccer World Cup.

The variant of indoor soccer officially recognized by the FIFA is called futsal. The name is derived from the Portuguese term *futebol de salão* and the Spanish *fútbol sala* ("indoor soccer").

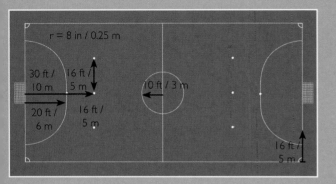

The playing field is limited by lines (handball field), not by edges, and is 125–138 × 68–82 ft / 38–42 × 20–25 m in size (for international match).

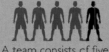

A team consists of five players (4 outfield players, 1 goalkeeper).

Substitutions are unlimited and immediate.

Playtime is two 20 minute periods.

Handball goals are played.

The throw-in is replaced by a kick-in.

The penalty kick is executed from 20 ft / 6 m distance.

Bounce-reduced ball: Circumference of 24–25 in / 62–64 cm (a standard ball measures 27–28 in / 68–70 cm), 8.7–13 psi / 0.6–0.9 bar excess pressure (8.7–16 psi / 0.6–1.1 bar excess pressure for a standard soccer ball).

From a 7-in / 2-m drop, the ball may not bounce lower than 20 in / 50 cm, and no higher than 26 in / 65 cm.

Beach soccer is played at the beach or on sand.

The game is played barefoot.

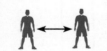

A team consists of five players (4 outfield players, 1 goalkeeper).

Substitutions are unlimited and immediate.

Playtime is three rounds of 12 minutes each. Changeovers take place after each round.

The 4-seconds rule applies: corner, kick-in, free kick, goal kick, ball possession, and ball control of the goalkeeper in one's own penalty box all must be played within 4 seconds.

There is no wall during a free kick.

FIFA

FIFA is short for Fédération Internationale de Football Association (International Federation of Association Football). It was founded in 1904 by Carl Anton Wilhelm Hirschmann (NL) and Robert Guérin (F) in Paris.

FIFA is the soccer world federation.

Official languages:
German, English, French, and Spanish
Conference language: English

Since 1923 the FIFA headquarters are in Zurich.

Founding members:
National soccer associations of Switzerland, Denmark, France, the Netherlands, Belgium, Sweden and Spain (back then represented by Madrid Football Club, today Real Madrid). The German soccer association joined by telegram.

First matches:
1908 Summer Olympics
1930 first soccer World Cup

FIFA conference

Highest decision-making body: annual meetings take place since 1998

Makes decisions on bylaws
Elects the FIFA president
Decides on the admittance and suspension of a member
1 vote per national association
(209, effective: January 2016)

Official language:
German, English, French, Spanish, Arabic, Portuguese, Russian
Conference language: English

Executive committee

Chair
President

25 members

President

8 vice-presidents

16 members

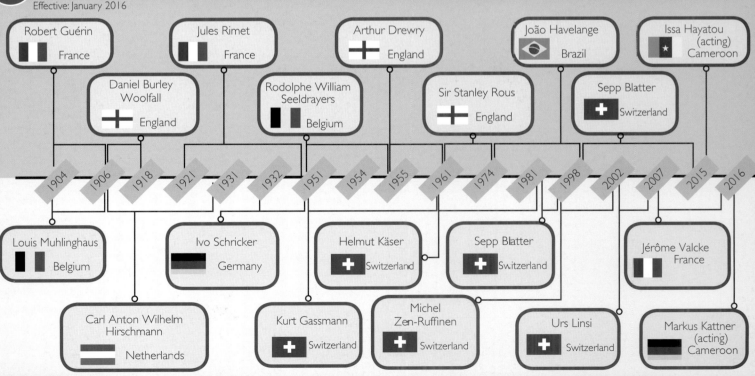

Effective: January 2016

FIFA presidents

Robert Guérin — France
Jules Rimet — France
Arthur Drewry — England
João Havelange — Brazil
Issa Hayatou (acting) — Cameroon
Daniel Burley Woolfall — England
Rodolphe William Seeldrayers — Belgium
Sir Stanley Rous — England
Sepp Blatter — Switzerland

1904 · 1906 · 1918 · 1921 · 1931 · 1932 · 1951 · 1954 · 1955 · 1961 · 1974 · 1981 · 1998 · 2002 · 2007 · 2015 · 2016

FIFA secretary generals

Louis Muhlinghaus — Belgium
Ivo Schricker — Germany
Helmut Käser — Switzerland
Sepp Blatter — Switzerland
Jérôme Valcke — France
Carl Anton Wilhelm Hirschmann — Netherlands
Kurt Gassmann — Switzerland
Michel Zen-Ruffinen — Switzerland
Urs Linsi — Switzerland
Markus Kattner (acting) — Cameroon

FIFA organizes the following matches:

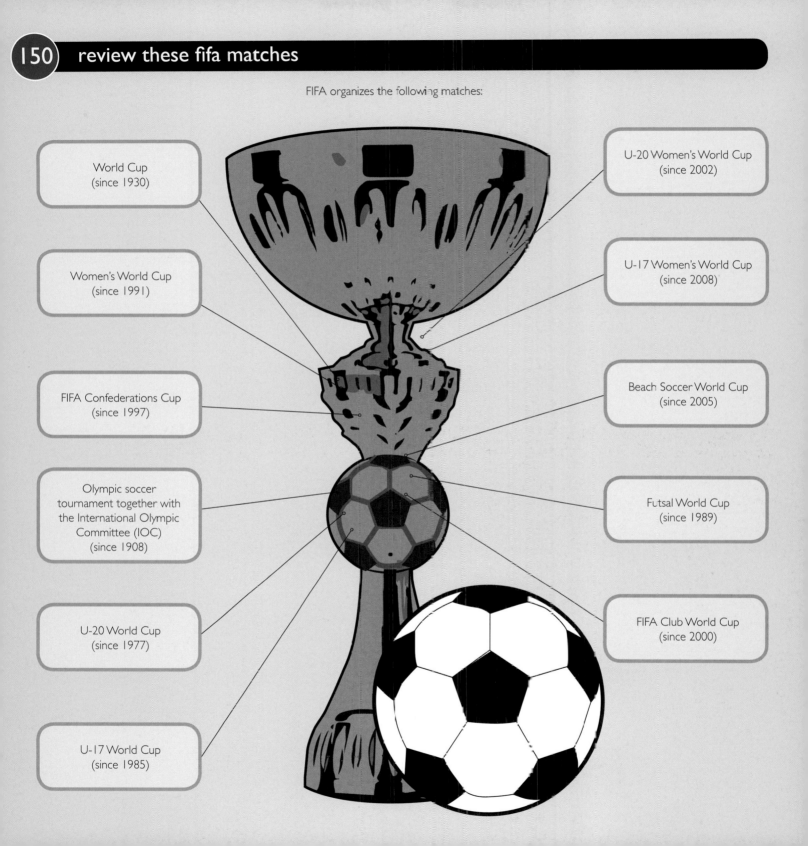

World Cup
(since 1930)

Women's World Cup
(since 1991)

FIFA Confederations Cup
(since 1997)

Olympic soccer
tournament together with
the International Olympic
Committee (IOC)
(since 1908)

U-20 World Cup
(since 1977)

U-17 World Cup
(since 1985)

U-20 Women's World Cup
(since 2002)

U-17 Women's World Cup
(since 2008)

Beach Soccer World Cup
(since 2005)

Futsal World Cup
(since 1989)

FIFA Club World Cup
(since 2000)

Every 4 years

Played by national teams

Organizer: FIFA
All teams that have successfully qualified worldwide, as well as the team of the host country, play for the silverware.

Group stage

8 groups with 4 teams

In the group phase each team plays agains the other three teams of the group (3 games for each team).

Victory:
3 points

Tie:
1 point

Defeat:
no points

The two last-placed teams are eliminated.
Decision at level score:
• Goal difference
• Higher number of goals
• Direct comparison between the two teams (points/goal differences/higher number of goals)
At a tie: Draw

Winners

Second place

16 teams remain.

Other rounds

These are played following the single-elimination system—only the winner goes through.

At a tie: Overtime **044** understand overtime   **At a tie or after overtime:** Penalty shootout **045** see a penalty shootout

Last sixteen
Each top team plays against the second-best team of another group (8 matches).

8 teams remain.

Quarter finals
The winners play one of the four quarter final matches.

4 teams remain

Semifinals
The winners move forward to one of the two semifinals.

Small final
The two losing teams of the semifinals battle for third place in the "small final".

3.

Final
The two winning teams play in the final for the World Cup. The winning team receives the cup.

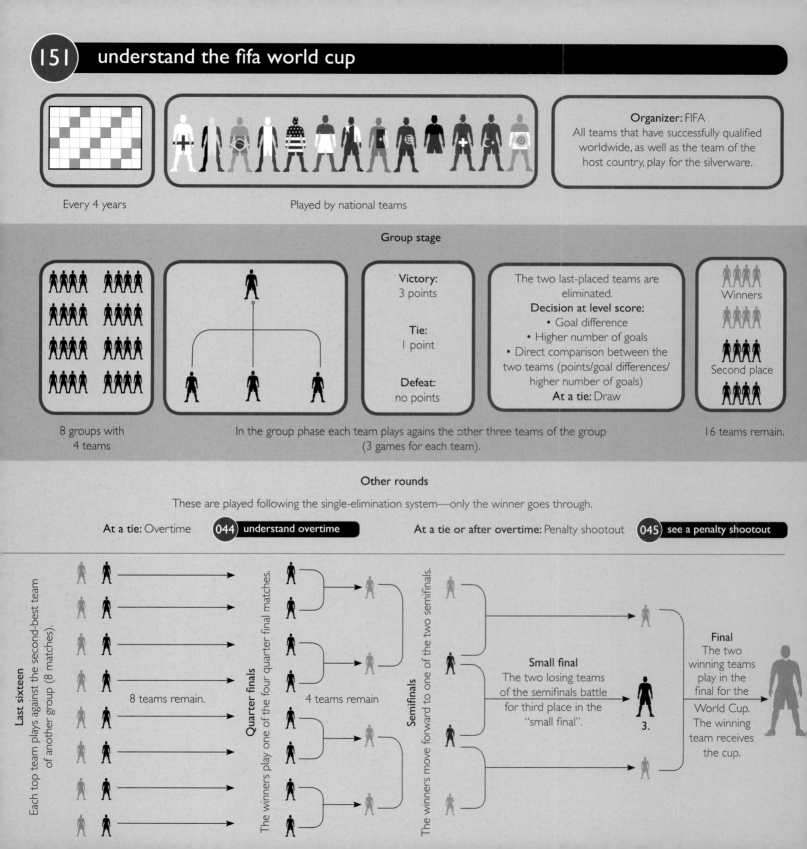

get familiar with fifa continental associations and confederations

All associations organize qualifiers for the World Cup and the Olympics.

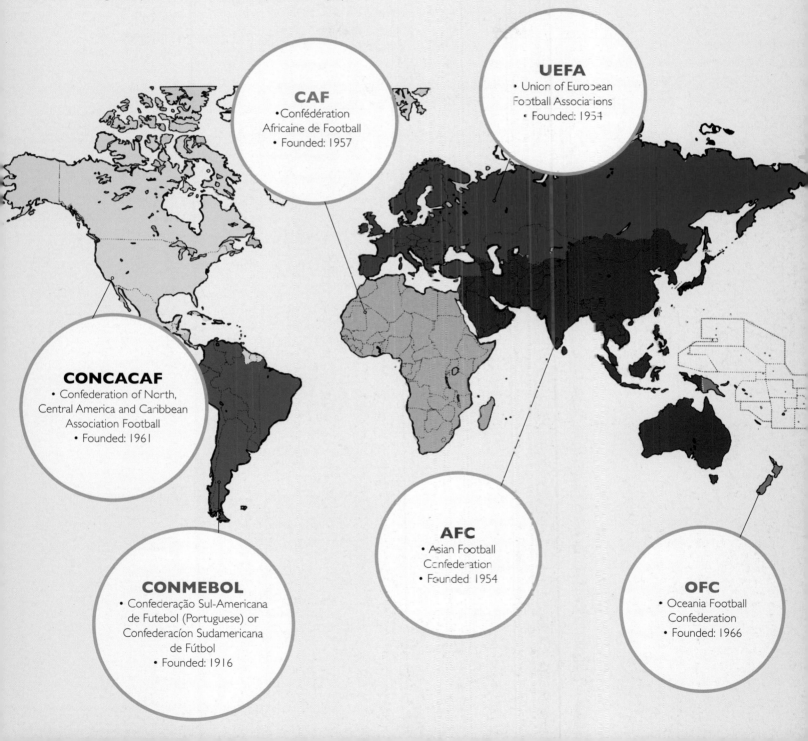

CAF
- Confédération Africaine de Football
- Founded: 1957

UEFA
- Union of European Football Associations
- Founded: 1954

CONCACAF
- Confederation of North, Central America and Caribbean Association Football
- Founded: 1961

CONMEBOL
- Confederação Sul-Americana de Futebol (Portuguese) or Confederacíon Sudamericana de Fútbol
- Founded: 1916

AFC
- Asian Football Confederation
- Founded: 1954

OFC
- Oceania Football Confederation
- Founded: 1966

Host: Uruguay
Winner: Uruguay
2nd place: Argentina
3rd place: USA

1930

Host: Italy
Winner: Italy
2nd place: Czechoslovakia
3rd place: German Reich (Nazi era) Germany

1934

Host: France
Winner: Italy
2nd place: Hungary
3rd place: Brazil

1938

Host: Brazil
Winner: Uruguay
2nd place: Brazil
3rd place: Sweden

1950

Host: France
Winner: France
2nd place: Brazil
3rd place: Croatia

1998

Host: USA
Winner: Brazil
2nd place: Italy
3rd place: Sweden

1994

Host: Italy
Winner: West Germany
2nd place: Argentina
3rd place: Italy

1990

Host: Mexico
Winner: Argentina
2nd place West Germany
3rd place: France

1986

Host: Japan and South Korea
Winner: Brazil
2nd place: Germany
3rd place: Turkey

2002

Host: Germany
Winner: Italy
2nd place: France
3rd place: Germany

2006

Host: South Africa
Winner: Spain
2nd place: Netherlands
3rd place: Germany

2010

Host: Brazil
Winner: Germany
2nd place: Argentina
3rd place: Netherlands

2014

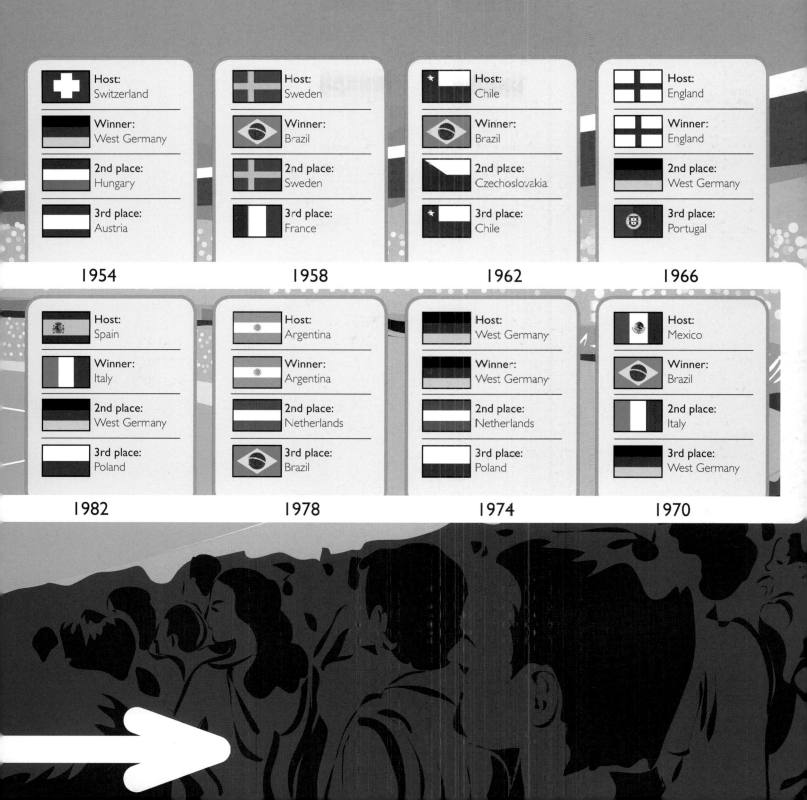

Host:
Switzerland

Winner:
West Germany

2nd place:
Hungary

3rd place:
Austria

1954

Host:
Sweden

Winner:
Brazil

2nd place:
Sweden

3rd place:
France

1958

Host:
Chile

Winner:
Brazil

2nd place:
Czechoslovakia

3rd place:
Chile

1962

Host:
England

Winner:
England

2nd place:
West Germany

3rd place:
Portugal

1966

Host:
Spain

Winner:
Italy

2nd place:
West Germany

3rd place:
Poland

1982

Host:
Argentina

Winner:
Argentina

2nd place:
Netherlands

3rd place:
Brazil

1978

Host:
West Germany

Winner:
West Germany

2nd place:
Netherlands

3rd place:
Poland

1974

Host:
Mexico

Winner:
Brazil

2nd place:
Italy

3rd place:
West Germany

1970

Brazil 5 times

(West) Germany 4 times

Italy 4 times

Argentina 2 times

Uruguay 2 times

England 1 time

France 1 time

Spain 1 time

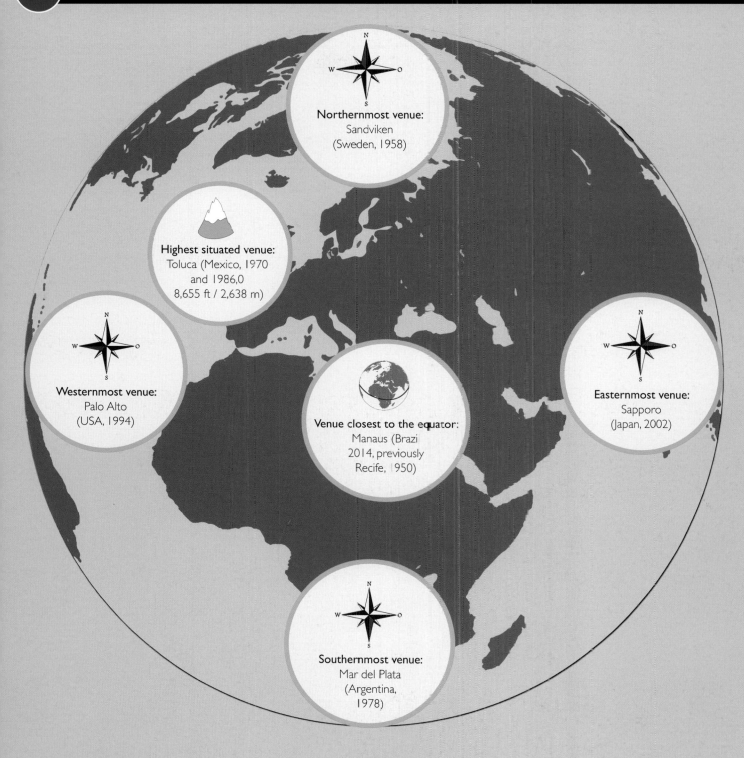

Northernmost venue:
Sandviken
(Sweden, 1958)

Highest situated venue:
Toluca (Mexico, 1970
and 1986,0
8,655 ft / 2,638 m)

Westernmost venue:
Palo Alto
(USA, 1994)

Venue closest to the equator:
Manaus (Brazi
2014, previously
Recife, 1950)

Easternmost venue:
Sapporo
(Japan, 2002)

Southernmost venue:
Mar del Plata
(Argentina,
1978)

So far there has only been one match that ended with a double-digit score in the history of the World Cup:
In 1982 the Hungarian national team sent El Salvador home 10-1.

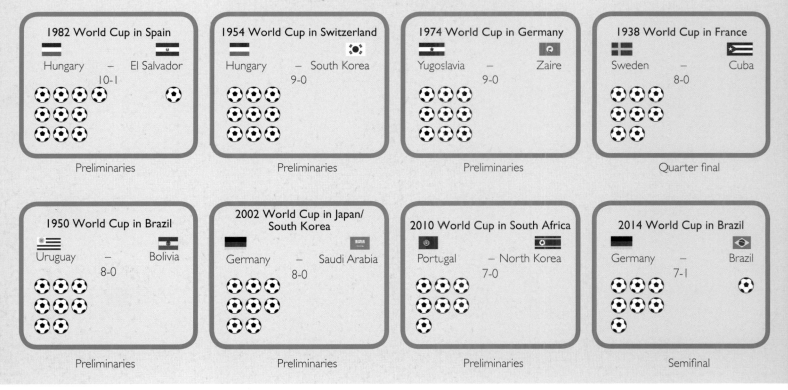

1982 World Cup in Spain
Hungary – El Salvador
10-1
Preliminaries

1954 World Cup in Switzerland
Hungary – South Korea
9-0
Preliminaries

1974 World Cup in Germany
Yugoslavia – Zaire
9-0
Preliminaries

1938 World Cup in France
Sweden – Cuba
8-0
Quarter final

1950 World Cup in Brazil
Uruguay – Bolivia
8-0
Preliminaries

2002 World Cup in Japan/South Korea
Germany – Saudi Arabia
8-0
Preliminaries

2010 World Cup in South Africa
Portugal – North Korea
7-0
Preliminaries

2014 World Cup in Brazil
Germany – Brazil
7-1
Semifinal

12 goals:
Austria – Switzerland 7-5 at the 1954 World
Cup quarter final (heat battle of Lausanne)

11 goals:
Hungary – El Salvador 10-1 (preliminaries 1982),
Hungary – Germany 8-3 (preliminaries 1954),
Brazil – Poland 6-5 AET (last sixteen 1938)

10 goals:
France – Paraguay 7-3 (preliminares 1958)

1. Cup 1930

1 goal
Lucien Laurent, 1930, scored the first World Cup goal. His record lasted 83 minutes.

2 goals
André Maschinot, 1930, scored two goals in the same match. His record lasted 4 days.

3 goals
Ivan Bek, 1930, scored three goals in two matches. His record lasted 53 minutes.

4 goals
Bertram Patenaude, 1930, scored four goals in two matches. His record lasted five days.

8 goals
Guillermo Stàbile, 1930, scored eight goals in four matches and was also the first World Cup topscorer. His record lasted nearly 20 years.

9 goals
Ademir, 1950, scored nine goals in six matches. His record lasted roughly four years.

11 goals
Sándor Kocsis, 1954, was the first player who scored more than ten goals in a World Cup. His record lasted roughly four years.

12 goals
However, Pelé and Jürgen Klinsmann scored their goals in several tournaments.

13 goals
Just Fontaine, 1958, scored 13 goals in six matches. His record lasted about 16 years.

14 goals
Gerd Müller scored his goals in several tournaments. His record lasted almost 32 years.

15 goals
Ronaldo scored his goals in three tournaments. His record lasted eight years.

16 goals
Miroslav Klose scored his goals in four tournaments. He has been holding this record since 2014.

First World Cup goal
Lucien Laurent (France) after 19 minutes against Mexico at the **1930 World Cup**

The most goals in the shortest amount of time Germany
4 goals in 6 minutes

Final score: Germany against Brazil 7-1, **2014 World Cup**

The most goals in a World Cup tournament
Just Fontaine (France) 13 scores

in 6 encounters at the **1958 World Cup**

The most goals in one game
Oleg Salenko (Russia—5 goals in the match against Cameroon,

Final score: 6-1 at the **1994 World Cup**

The most headed goals in a World Cup tournament
Miroslav Klose (Germany) —5 out of 5 scores through headers in 7 encounters

at the **2002 World Cup**

First player
with at least four goals in three World Cups each:
Miroslav Klose:
2002 (5),
2006 (5),
2010 (4)

First player
with at least three goals in three World Cups each:
Jürgen Klinsmann:
1990 (3),
1994 (5),
1998 (3)

The most goals in total
Germany
(224),

The most goals against in total
Germany
(121)

First player
with at least two goals in four World Cups each:
Uwe Seeler:
1958 (2),
1962 (2),
1966 (2)
and 1970 (3)

First golden goal in a World Cup:
Laurent Blanc (France) in the last sixteen at the **1998 World Cup** against Paraguay leading to 1-0 for France.

The least goals in total
Angola (2)

only participation in a final in 2006, only three preliminaries

First "flawless" hat-trick:
Edmund Conen (Germany) 1934 in the match against Belgium, final score 5-2.

The most games without a goal against
Peter Shilton (1982–1990) (England) and **Fabien Barthez** (1998–2006) (France)—10

160 perform at the last minute

These penalty kicks were each performed in the last minutes of play.

1962 World Cup
Mexico–USSR leading to 3-1 for Mexico

1974 World Cup
West Germany–Sweden leading to 4-2 for Germany

1994 World Cup
Argentina–Greece leading to 4-0 for Argentina

1998 World Cup
South Africa–Saudi-Arabia leading to 2-2, but the score was no longer relevant to go through to the next round.

1998 World Cup
Italy–Austria, getting one back for Austria leading to 2-1

2010 World Cup
Uruguay–Ghana (quarter final) at the last minute of the added time of the overtime at the score of 1-1. Asamoah Gyan, who had converted two penalty kicks in the first round, missed and in the following penalty shootout Ghana lost at 2-4, but Gyan converted the first penalty kick for Ghana.

2014 World Cup
Greece–Ivory Coast, Giorgos Samaras converted in the 93rd minute to a 2-1 for Greece, which made it to the last sixteen instead of the Ivory Coast.

Netherlands–Mexico (last sixteen) Klaas-Jan Huntelaar scores in the 94th minute leading to the 2-1 match winner.

2002 World Cup
Spain–Ireland (last sixteen) leading to the 1-1 equalizer for Ireland, Spain reached the quarter final through the penalty shootout.

2010 World Cup
Netherlands–Slovakia (last sixteen) in the 3rd minute of the added time leading to getting back at 1-2 for Slovakia, the game was stopped immediately afterwards.

161 look at the fastest world cup goals

Hakan Sükür (Turkey) after 11 seconds in the match against South Korea in 2002

Václav Mašek (Czechoslovakia) after 15 seconds in the match against Mexico in 1962

Ernst Lehner (Germany) after 25 seconds in the match against Austria in 1934

check out the most world cup tournament goals

1930	Argentina	18 goals in 4 matches
1934	Italy	12 goals in 5 matches
1938	Hungary	15 goals in 4 matches
1950	Brazil	22 goals in 6 matches
1954	Hungary	27 goals in 5 matches
1958	France	23 goals in 6 matches
1962	Brazil	14 goals in 6 matches

1966	Portugal	17 goals in 6 matches
1970	Brazil	19 goals in 6 matches
1974	Poland	16 goals in 7 matches
1978	Argentina	15 goals in 7 matches
1978	Netherlands	15 goals in 7 matches
1982	France	16 goals in 7 matches
1986	Argentina	14 goals in 7 matches

1990	West Germany	15 goals in 7 matches
1994	Sweden	15 goals in 7 matches
1998	France	15 goals in 7 matches
2002	Brazil	18 goals in 7 matches
2006	Germany	14 goals in 7 matches
2010	Germany	16 goals in 7 matches
2014	Germany	18 goals in 7 matches

look at the most world cup tournament goals against

1930	Mexico	13 goals in 3 matches
1934	Germany	8 goals in 4 matches
1938	Cuba	12 goals in 3 matches
1950	Sweden	15 goals in 5 matches
1954	South Korea	16 goals in 2 matches
1958	France	15 goals in 6 matches
1962	Columbia	11 goals in 3 matches
1966	Switzerland	9 goals in 3 matches
1966	North Korea	9 goals in 4 matches

1970	West Germany	10 goals in 6 matches
1974	Zaire	14 goals in 3 matches
1974	Haiti	14 goals in 3 matches
1978	Mexico	12 goals in 3 matches
	Peru	12 goals in 6 matches
1982	El Salvador	13 goals in 3 matches
1986	Belgium	15 goals in 7 matches
1990	United Arab Emirates	11 goals in 3 matches

1994	Cameroon	11 goals in 3 matches
	Bulgaria	11 goals in 7 matches
1998	Brazil	10 goals in 7 matches
2002	Saudi Arabia	12 goals in 3 matches
2006	Serbia	10 goals in 3 matches
2006	Montenegro	10 goals in 3 matches
2010	North Korea	12 goals in 3 matches
2014	Brazil	14 goals in 7 matches

164 meet the oldest world cup soccer veterans

In the preliminary round of Columbia versus Japan, the Columbian trainer Faryd Mondragon was brought in as goalkeeper. Mondragon was 43 years old at the time.

One of the most famous goals scorers is also one of the oldest in World Cup history: Roger Milla from Cameroon was 42 when he played in the 1994 World Cup in the USA.

The Italian goalkeeper Dino Zoff became world champion in 1982 at 40.

165 get to know the youngest world cup players

The youngest player who was deployed in a World Cup was Norman Whiteside (Northern Ireland). He played in the 1982 World Cup at the age of 17 years and 41 days.

The youngest World Cup goal scorer was Pelé (Brazil), who scored at the 1958 World Cup at the age of 17 years and 239 days.

At the age of 17 years and 249 days, Pelé also became the youngest world champion at the 1958 World Cup.

Adidas, Coca-Cola, Emirates, Hyundai/Kia, Sony, and Visa are permanent partners of FIFA. International World Cup sponsors, which can vary from one event to the other, as well as national sponsors, ensure further revenue.

Since the 1982 World Cup, FIFA has been selling exclusive marketing rights to companies which are then called "official sponsors of the World Cup" and are allowed to advertize with the World Cup logo and the FIFA brand. FIFA monitors closely that these affiliates are exclusively represented at the respective soccer stadium during a World Cup.

Adidas has been the official partner of FIFA for more than 40 years. The company dresses ball-boys, helpers, and referees; and supplies the match ball.

There are no official numbers concerning how much FIFA partners pay for their special rights. But in business circles it is said that each sponsor pays roughly 50 million euro.

The stars are awarded by soccer clubs and organizations for trophies won and are attached to the shirts. The criteria for awarding stars differ depending on the country and competition.

Women's World Cup stars

National team	Stars	Year of World Cup trophies won
USA		1991, 1999, 2015
Germany	✦ ✦	2003, 2007
Norway		1995
Japan	✦	2011

Men's World Cup stars

National team	Stars	Year of World Cup trophies won
Brazil		1958, 1962, 1970, 1994, 2002
Germany	✦ ✦ ✦ ✦	1954, 1974, 1990, 2014
Italy		1934, 1938, 1982, 2006
Uruguay	✦ ✦	1930, 1950
Argentina		1978, 1986
England	✦	1966
France		1998
Spain	✦	2010

The first official international cap in the history of soccer took place at Hamilton Crescent near Glasgow where a Scottish and an English team faced each other.

Final score: 0-0

1872

The Austria–Switzerland match in 1901 is called the "ur-international cap" but is not officially an international cap.

Final score: 0-4

1901

The first official international cap that featured two non-British teams (Uruguay–Argentina in Montevideo) was also the first international cap outside of Europe.

Final score: 0-6

1902

The first official international cap between Germany and Switzerland took place in 1908.

Final score: 3-5

1908

The first official international cap between Switzerland and France took place in 1905.

Final score: 0-1

1905

The first international cap between two non-British European teams: Austria–Hungary in Vienna

Final score: 5-0

1902

The first international cap between a European and a non-European team: Sweden–USA

Final score: 2-3

1916

The first international cap between a European and an African team: Italy–Egypt.

Final score: 2-1

1920

The first international cap between a European and a South American team (Uruguay–Yugoslavia) during the Olympic Games

Final score: 7-0

1924

The Miracle of Bern, 1954

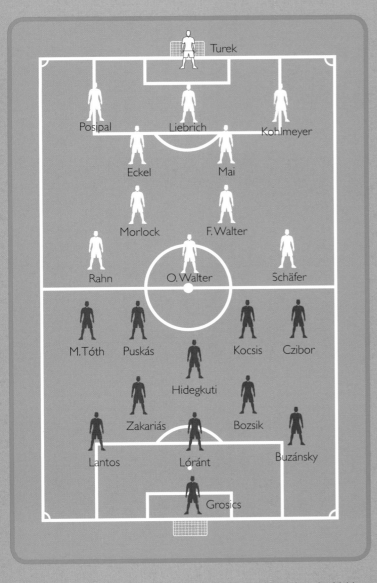

The Wembley Goal, 1966

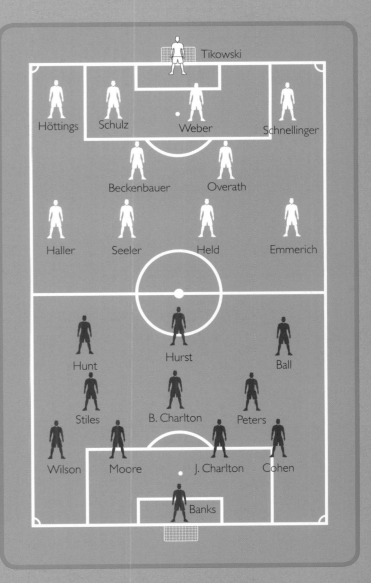

In the 1954 World Cup in Switzerland, Germany won against the highly favored Hungarian national team. This victory is called the Miracle of Bern. The players around captain Fritz Walter and national coach Sepp Herberger went down in German sports history as the "Heroes of Bern."

In the World Cup final Germany versus England, the score stood at 1-1 after 20 minutes; England took the lead 12 minutes before the end of the match, but Weber managed to equalize the score in overtime. Geoff Hurst scored the controversial Wembley goal in the 101st minute: The ball bounced off the bottom edge of the crossbar and flew back onto, behind, or in front of the goalline. To this day, opinions differ as to whether this was a goal or not.

The Miracle of Córdoba, 1978

The Miracle of Istanbul, 2005

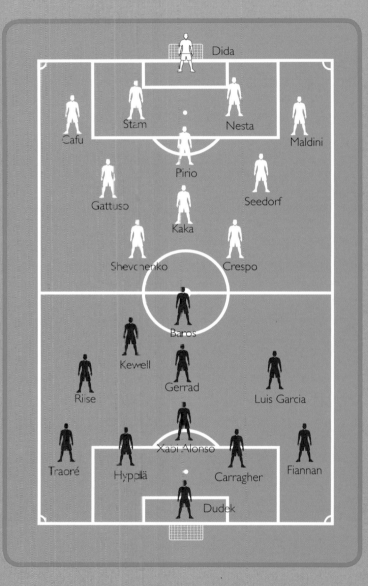

The match, known in Austria as the "Miracle of Córdoba"—in Germany known as the "Disgrace of Córdoba"—was the last match of the intermediate stage of the 1978 World Cup in Córdoba, Argentina, between Austria and Germany. The German team lost as the reigning world champion against Austria 2-3. The result was irrelevant for the course of the tournament; both teams were eliminated after the match.

The 2005 Champions League final is known as the "comeback of the century," and is often called the "Miracle of Istanbul." After a 0-3 halftime advantage for AC Milan, FC Liverpool leveled the score within only six minutes to 3-3 and, in the end, won the match during the penalty shootout.

The winners of the Intercontinental Cup were only determined for 44 years, between 1960 and 2004.
This event was held between the winners of the Champions League and the Copa Libertadores (highlighted in blue).
The inofficial follow-up event is the Club World Cup organized by the FIFA.

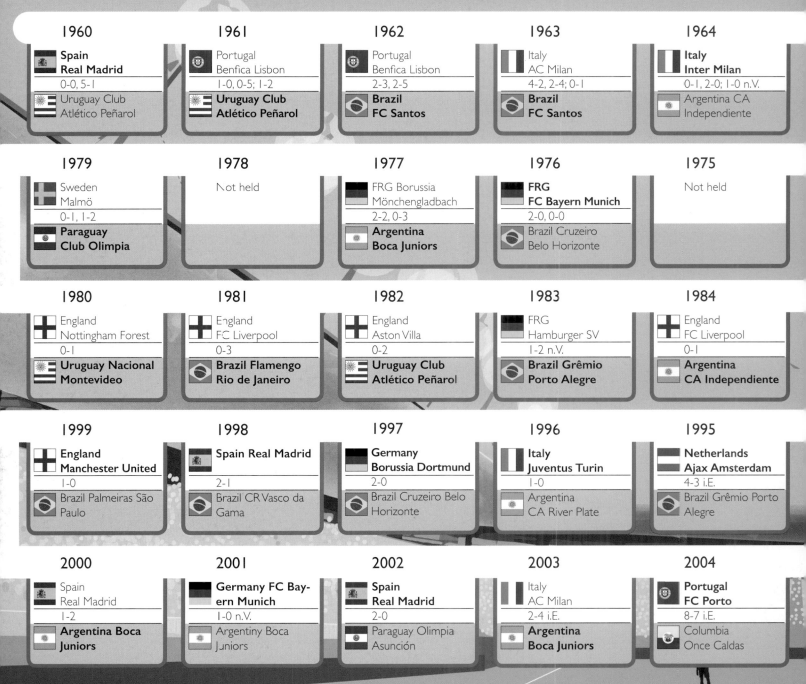

1960
Spain
Real Madrid
0-0, 5-1
Uruguay Club
Atlético Peñarol

1961
Portugal
Benfica Lisbon
1-0, 0-5; 1-2
Uruguay Club
Atlético Peñarol

1962
Portugal
Benfica Lisbon
2-3, 2-5
Brazil
FC Santos

1963
Italy
AC Milan
4-2, 2-4; 0-1
Brazil
FC Santos

1964
Italy
Inter Milan
0-1, 2-0; 1-0 n.V.
Argentina CA
Independiente

1979
Sweden
Malmö
0-1, 1-2
Paraguay
Club Olimpia

1978
Not held

1977
FRG Borussia
Mönchengladbach
2-2, 0-3
Argentina
Boca Juniors

1976
FRG
FC Bayern Munich
2-0, 0-0
Brazil Cruzeiro
Belo Horizonte

1975
Not held

1980
England
Nottingham Forest
0-1
Uruguay Nacional
Montevideo

1981
England
FC Liverpool
0-3
Brazil Flamengo
Rio de Janeiro

1982
England
Aston Villa
0-2
Uruguay Club
Atlético Peñarol

1983
FRG
Hamburger SV
1-2 n.V.
Brazil Grêmio
Porto Alegre

1984
England
FC Liverpool
0-1
Argentina
CA Independiente

1999
England
Manchester United
1-0
Brazil Palmeiras São
Paulo

1998
Spain Real Madrid
2-1
Brazil CR Vasco da
Gama

1997
Germany
Borussia Dortmund
2-0
Brazil Cruzeiro Belo
Horizonte

1996
Italy
Juventus Turin
1-0
Argentina
CA River Plate

1995
Netherlands
Ajax Amsterdam
4-3 i.E.
Brazil Grêmio Porto
Alegre

2000
Spain
Real Madrid
1-2
Argentina Boca
Juniors

2001
Germany FC Bay-
ern Munich
1-0 n.V.
Argentiny Boca
Juniors

2002
Spain
Real Madrid
2-0
Paraguay Olimpia
Asunción

2003
Italy
AC Milan
2-4 i.E.
Argentina
Boca Juniors

2004
Portugal
FC Porto
8-7 i.E.
Columbia
Once Caldas

1965

Italy
Inter Milan
3-0, 0-0
Argentina CA
Independiente

1966

Spain
Real Madrid
0-2, 0-2
**Uruguay Club
Atlético Peñarol**

1967

Scotland
Celtic Glasgow
1-0, 1-2; 0-1 1
**Argentina
Racing Club
Avellaneda**

1968

England
Manchester United
0-1, 1-1
**Argentina
Estudiantes
de La Plata**

1969

Italiy
AC Milan
3-0, 1-2
Argentina
Estudiantes
de La Plata

1974

Spain
Atlético Madrid
0-1, 2-0
Argentina CA
Independiente

1973

Italy
Juventus Turin
0-1
**Argentina CA
Independiente**

1972

Netherlands
Ajax Amsterdam
1-1, 3-0
Argentina CA
Independiente

1971

Greece
Panathinaikos Athens
1-1, 1-2
**Uruguay Nacional
Montevideo**

1970

Netherlands
Feyenoord Rotterdam
2-2, 1-0
Argentina
Estudiantes
de La Plata

1985

Italy
Juventus Turin
6-4 i.E.
Argentina
Argentinos Juniors

1986

Rumania
Steaua Bucharest
0-1
**Argentina CA
River Plate**

1987

Portugal
FC Porto
2-1 n.V.
Uruguay Club
Atlético Peñarol

1988

Netherlands
PSV Eindhoven
6-7 i.E.
Uruguay Nacional
Montevideo

1989

Italy
AC Milan
1-0 n.V.
Columbia Atlético
Nacional

1994

Italy
AC Milan
0-2
**Argentina
CA Vélez Sársfield**

1993

Italy
AC Milan 9
2-3
**Brazil FC São
Paulo**

1992

Spain
FC Barcelona
1-2
**Brazil
FC São Paulo**

1991

Yugoslavia
Red Star Belgrade
3-0
Chile
CSD Colo-Colo

1990

Italy
AC Milan
3-0
Paraguay Club
Olimpia

Men's Olympic Soccer Tournaments

Gold: Great Britain	
Silver: France	
Bronze: Belgium	

1900 London *

Gold: Canada	
Silver: USA	
Bronze: USA	

1904 St. Louis **

Gold: Denmark	
Silver/Bronze: Ottoman Empire	

1906 Athens (intermediate matches) *******

Gold: Great Britain	
Silver: Denmark	
Bronze: Netherlands	

1908 London

Gold: Poland	
Silver: Hungary	
Bronze: Soviet Union, GDR	

1972 Munich ****

Gold: Hungary	
Silver: Bulgaria	
Bronze: Japan	

1968 Mexico City

Gold: Hungary	
Silver: Czechoslovakia	
Bronze: West Germany	

1964 Tokyo

Gold: Yugoslavia	
Silver: Denmark	
Bronze: Hungary	

1960 Rome

Gold: GDR	
Silver: Poland	
Bronze: Soviet Union	

1976 Montreal

Gold: Czechoslovakia	
Silver: GDR	
Bronze: Soviet Union	

1980 Moscow

Gold: France	
Silver: Brazil	
Bronze: Yugoslavia	

1984 Los Angeles

Gold: Soviet Union	
Silver: Brazil	
Bronze: West Germany	

1988 Seoul

Gold: Mexico	
Silver: Brazil	
Bronze: South Korea	

2012 London

Gold: USA	
Silver: Japan	
Bronze: Canada	

Gold: Argentina	
Silver: Nigeria	
Bronze: Brazil	

Gold: USA	
Silver: Brazil	
Bronze: Germany	

2008 Beijing

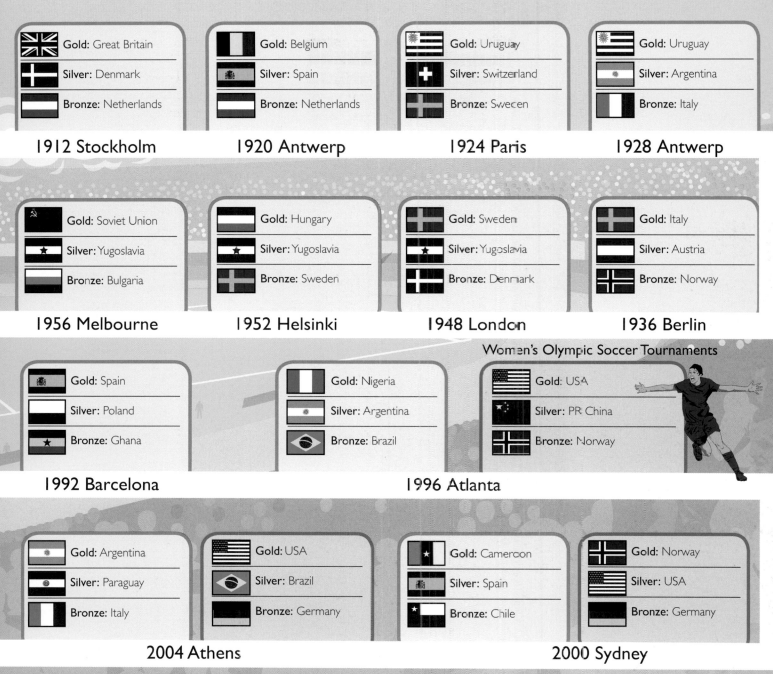

1912 Stockholm
- **Gold:** Great Britain
- **Silver:** Denmark
- **Bronze:** Netherlands

1920 Antwerp
- **Gold:** Belgium
- **Silver:** Spain
- **Bronze:** Netherlands

1924 Paris
- **Gold:** Uruguay
- **Silver:** Switzerland
- **Bronze:** Sweden

1928 Antwerp
- **Gold:** Uruguay
- **Silver:** Argentina
- **Bronze:** Italy

1956 Melbourne
- **Gold:** Soviet Union
- **Silver:** Yugoslavia
- **Bronze:** Bulgaria

1952 Helsinki
- **Gold:** Hungary
- **Silver:** Yugoslavia
- **Bronze:** Sweden

1948 London
- **Gold:** Sweden
- **Silver:** Yugoslavia
- **Bronze:** Denmark

1936 Berlin
- **Gold:** Italy
- **Silver:** Austria
- **Bronze:** Norway

1992 Barcelona
- **Gold:** Spain
- **Silver:** Poland
- **Bronze:** Ghana

1996 Atlanta
- **Gold:** Nigeria
- **Silver:** Argentina
- **Bronze:** Brazil

Women's Olympic Soccer Tournaments
- **Gold:** USA
- **Silver:** PR China
- **Bronze:** Norway

2004 Athens
- **Gold:** Argentina
- **Silver:** Paraguay
- **Bronze:** Italy

- **Gold:** USA
- **Silver:** Brazil
- **Bronze:** Germany

2000 Sydney
- **Gold:** Cameroon
- **Silver:** Spain
- **Bronze:** Chile

- **Gold:** Norway
- **Silver:** USA
- **Bronze:** Germany

(*) In 1900 two single matches took place between club teams. The IOC determined the ranking list in retrospect.
(**) In 1904 three club or school teams participated.
(***) Intermediate matches not recognized by the IOC in 1906. Four partially mixed teams participated, among these a city team from Copenhagen.
(****) In 1972 two bronze medals were awarded because the match for third place between the GDR and the USSR was still 2-2 even after overtime. Penalty shootouts were not performed at the time.

In the 19th century, players wore boots, not to create an advantage, but rather to protect them from possible injuries—sturdy brogues were often used as soccer boots. The boots were fitted with steel toes; the studs were intended to help in the frequently unfavorable conditions. The boots ended above the ankle. They were made of 100 percent leather and weighed roughly 1 lb / 500 g—in wet conditions they could easily weigh up to 2 lbs / 1 kg.

After the Second World War, more and more soccer boots were produced to create an advantage for the player on the field. The first screw-in studs were manufactured in Europe.

Today, soccer boots are made of synthetic material and are high-tech tools.

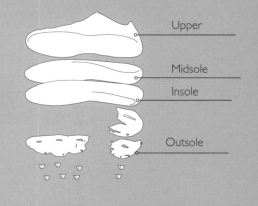

Upper

Midsole

Insole

Outsole

In the 1960s and 1970s, boots with a low rise were fashioned for the first time, which allowed for more mobility of the player.

173 compare the types of studs

Studs are a regular feature of the soles. The soccer boot needs to have at least ten studs.

The texture of the studs may not pose a risk of injury to the wearer or the opponent.

Nowadays there is a range of studs that are designed for specific areas of use. They differ not only in terms of material but also in terms of size, length, number, and positioning:

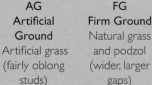

AG Artificial Ground	FG Firm Ground	HG Hard Ground	IN Indoor	SG Soft Ground	TF Turf
Artificial grass (fairly oblong studs)	Natural grass and podzol (wider, larger gaps)	Hard soil and podzol	Hall floor (no studs, treaded sole)	For heavy, moist ground (classic studs)	For hard soil, podzol, artificial grass (many small studs), called centipede

Originally made of cotton, most soccer shirts today are polyester breathable, and easy to clean. Professional shirts are often made of a lighter, finer mesh material.

Back:
Number (in the middle and clearly legible, 8–14 in / 20–35 cm high), player's name (above the number, 2–3 in / 5–7.5 cm high, 1.5 in / 4 cm distance to the number), possibly advertisement

Front:
Number (chest height, 4–6 in /10–15 cm high), club name/partner association/national flag (chest height), possibly advertisement on chest (31 in²/ 200 cm² maximum), stars

Pants:
Number (left or right pant leg, 4–6 in / 10–15 cm high), emblem/ national flag, stars

Socks:
Center front national flag, association, stars

Ravshan Ermatov (1977–), Uzbekistan, is the referee with the most World Cup matches since the 2014 World Cup (9).

Wolf-Dieter Ahlenfelder (1944–2014), Germany, headed the Bundesliga match between Werder Bremen and Hannover 96 half-drunk in 1975, and blew the whistle to end the first halftime after 32 minutes—though the linesman was able to convince him to continue the match, he still ended the first halftime 90 seconds too early.

Valentin Ivanov (1961–), Russia, European Championship referee in 2004 and at the 2006 World Cup, handed out the most sending-offs at a World Cup match (4).

Rudolf Kreitlein (1919–2012), Germany, formerly West Germany, World Cup referee in 1966, had the Argentinian team's captain dragged off the field by the police.

Ken Aston (1915–2001), England, introduced the yellow and red cards after the match headed by Kreitlein. They were first used in the 1970 World Cup.

Gottfried Dienst (1919–1998), Switzerland, referee of the World Cup final in 1966, called the as of yet hotly debated Wembley goal a goal.

Bibiana Steinhaus (1979–), Germany, was the first woman to blow the whistle in a match of the second Bundesliga during the 2007/2008 season. During the 2012 Olympics, she headed both the Women's World Cup final and the women's final.

The referee whistles at the beginning of a match, at a time out, at the continuation, and at the end of the match.

176 understand the referee whistle

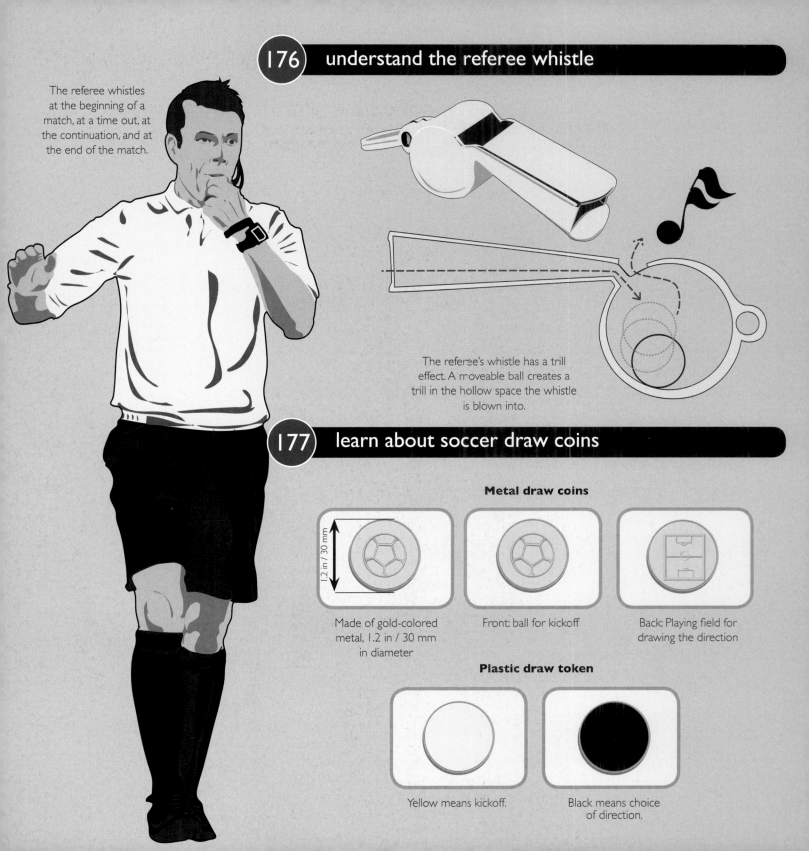

The referee's whistle has a trill effect. A moveable ball creates a trill in the hollow space the whistle is blown into.

177 learn about soccer draw coins

Metal draw coins

1.2 in / 30 mm

Made of gold-colored metal, 1.2 in / 30 mm in diameter

Front: ball for kickoff

Back: Playing field for drawing the direction

Plastic draw token

Yellow means kickoff.

Black means choice of direction.

(039) understand a sending-off / red card

(038) understand a warning / yellow card

The cards
are made of
polystyrene or
polyvinyl chloride.
Their corners are
rounded off.

The most red cards
The referee Jose Manuel Barro Escandon showed 19 red cards in a match between Recreativo Linense and Saladilo Algesiras in the Andalusian amateur league—but only in retrospect after the game was called off.

The fastest red card
The winner in this inglorious event is Walter Boyd. He received a red card after zero seconds in the match FC Swansea versus Darlington (1999). When his club, FC Swansea, was given a free kick, Boyd was sent in and rammed his elbow into an opponent's face.

The second-fastest red card
David Pratt, of the British seventh-leaguers Chippenham Town, was shown the red card three seconds after kickoff, when he violently attacked an opponent.

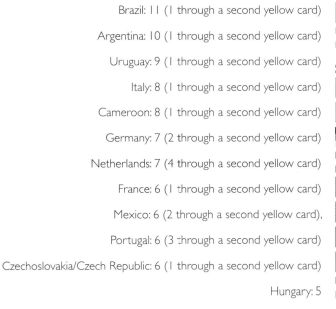
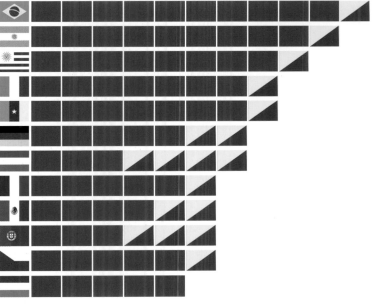

Brazil: 11 (1 through a second yellow card)

Argentina: 10 (1 through a second yellow card)

Uruguay: 9 (1 through a second yellow card)

Italy: 8 (1 through a second yellow card)

Cameroon: 8 (1 through a second yellow card)

Germany: 7 (2 through a second yellow card)

Netherlands: 7 (4 through a second yellow card)

France: 6 (1 through a second yellow card)

Mexico: 6 (2 through a second yellow card),

Portugal: 6 (3 through a second yellow card)

Czechoslovakia/Czech Republic: 6 (1 through a second yellow card)

Hungary: 5

180 learn about referee (mis)judgements

169 relive legendary matches

The Wembley Goal
1966 World Cup in
England,
Germany–England, 4-2
Was the ball behind the
line or not? The referee
decides it was a goal.

The Thriller of Sevilla
1982 World Cup Spain,
Germany–France, 8-7
The German goalkeeper Toni
Schumacher seriously injures the
French player Patrick Battiston.
Schumacher doesn't even receive
a warning; he blocks two penalty
kicks in the first World Cup
match, which ends with a
penalty shootout.

The hand of God
1986 World Cup Mexico,
Argentina–England, 2-1
Maradona pushes the ball
into the goal with his hand.
The referee doesn't see it.

Revenge for Wembley
2010 World Cup South Africa,
Germany–England, 4-1
Frank Lampard (England) shoots,
the ball bounces off the crossbar,
behind the line, bounces back up
to the crossbar, and lands in front
of the line. The referee doesn't see
it land behind the line: no goal.

143 memorize soccer quotes

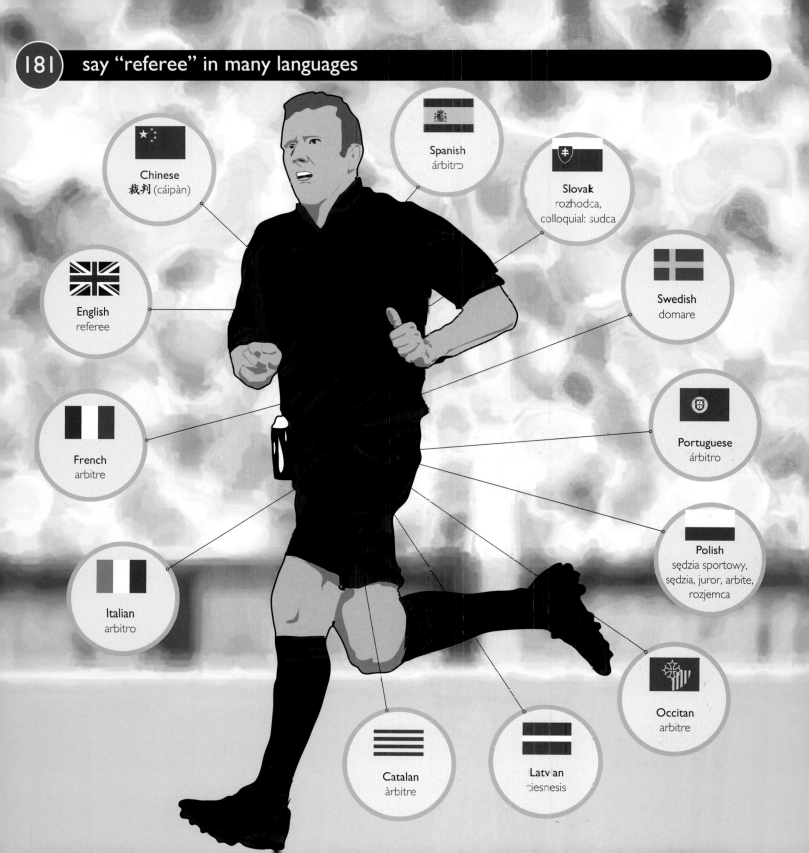

Chinese
裁判 (cáipàn)

Spanish
árbitro

Slovak
rozhodca,
colloquial: sudca

English
referee

Swedish
domare

French
arbitre

Portuguese
árbitro

Italian
arbitro

Polish
sędzia sportowy,
sędzia, juror, arbite,
rozjemca

Catalan
àrbitre

Latvian
tiesnesis

Occitan
arbitre

Men lie on the ground 30 seconds longer after a foul than women.

Men need ten seconds longer for substitutions than women.

Men celebrate a goal 30 seconds longer than women.

Men stall the game for tactical reasons more frequently than women.

The German national players received a 40-piece coffee set as a win bonus for winning the 1989 European championship.

Archie Thompson shot the most goals during an international cap. The Australian player scored 13 times in the 31-0 match against American Samoa.

Pelé
Brazil, 1956–1977
Position:
Striker
Strong points:
Dribbles, passes;
"best soccer player
of all time"

Johan Cruyff
Netherlands, 1964–1984
Position:
Midfield, striker
Strong point:
Highly talented
playmaker

Diego Maradona
Argentina, 1976–1997
Position:
Midfield
Strong points:
Inseparable from the
ball; perfect handling
of the ball

Alfredo di Stefano
Argentina, 1945–1966
Position:
Striker
Strong points:
Organizational skills

Ferenc Puskás
Hungary, 1942–1966
Position:
Striker
Strong points:
Strong and exact shots
with the left foot

Franz Beckenbauer
Germany, 1964–1983
Position:
Sweeper
Strong points:
Good team captain;
elegant and exact passes

Michel Platini
France, 1972–1988
Position:
Midfield
Strong point:
Free kick specialist

Eusebio
Portugal, 1957–1980
Position:
Midfield
Stärken:
Speed; strong and
exact shot

Lionel Messi
Argentina, 2003–
Position:
Wing, striker
Strong points:
Dribbles; speed;
exceptionally good
technique

Zinédine Zidane
France, 1988–2006
Position:
Midfield
Strong points:
Technically versed
all-rounder;
ball control

Marta Vieira da Silva
Brazil, 2002–
Position:
Striker
Strong points:
Exceptional speed;
ball handling; kicking
technique

Mia Hamm
USA, 2001–
Position:
Striker
Strong points:
Headers

Birgit Prinz
Germany, 1992–2013
Position:
Striker
Strong points:
Physical strength; shot
intensity

Abby Wambach
USA, 1999–2015
Position:
Striker
Strong point:
Non-conformist
play style

Homare Sawa
Japan, 1991–
Position:
Midfield
Strong points:
Ball circulation;
ball capturing;
ball possession

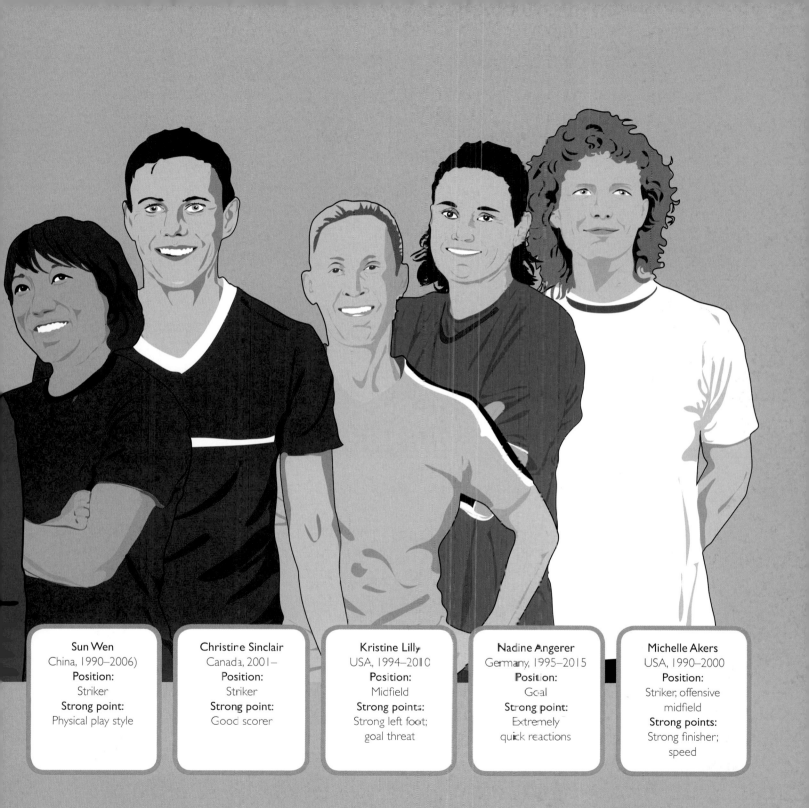

Sun Wen
China, 1990–2006)
Position:
Striker
Strong point:
Physical play style

Christine Sinclair
Canada, 2001–
Position:
Striker
Strong point:
Good scorer

Kristine Lilly
USA, 1994–2010
Position:
Midfield
Strong points:
Strong left foot;
goal threat

Nadine Angerer
Germany, 1995–2015
Position:
Goal
Strong point:
Extremely
quick reactions

Michelle Akers
USA, 1990–2000
Position:
Striker, offensive
midfield
Strong points:
Strong finisher;
speed

185 review the highest-income soccer clubs

Ranking 2015

Rank	Change Place	Country		Club	Earnings in €	
1.	±0	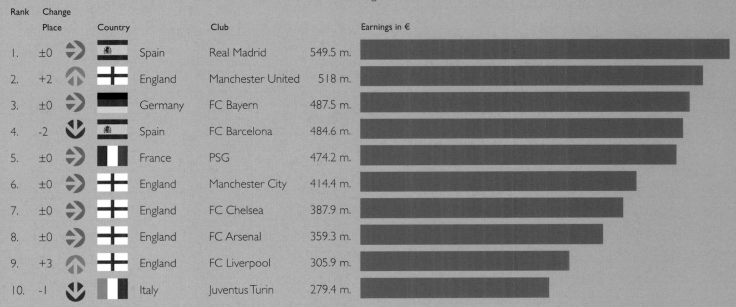	Spain	Real Madrid	549.5 m.	
2.	+2		England	Manchester United	518 m.	
3.	±0		Germany	FC Bayern	487.5 m.	
4.	-2		Spain	FC Barcelona	484.6 m.	
5.	±0		France	PSG	474.2 m.	
6.	±0		England	Manchester City	414.4 m.	
7.	±0		England	FC Chelsea	387.9 m.	
8.	±0		England	FC Arsenal	359.3 m.	
9.	+3		England	FC Liverpool	305.9 m.	
10.	-1		Italy	Juventus Turin	279.4 m.	

The Deloitte Football Money League is a ranking of the 20 worldwide high-ncome soccer clubs. t is pubished annually since 1998.
It gathers information on the earnings from proceeds on the actual matchdays (aud ence earnings etc.),
from broadcasting rights, advertising revenue, and revenue from royalties.

186 compare the 10 best-paid soccer trainers

Effective 2015

Annual salary in €

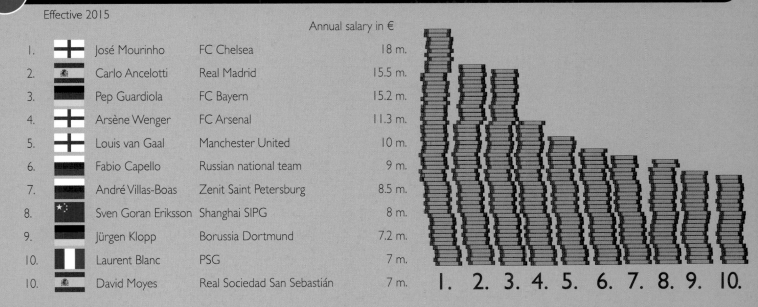

				Annual salary in €
1.		José Mourinho	FC Chelsea	18 m.
2.		Carlo Ancelotti	Real Madrid	15.5 m.
3.		Pep Guardiola	FC Bayern	15.2 m.
4.		Arsène Wenger	FC Arsenal	11.3 m.
5.		Louis van Gaal	Manchester United	10 m.
6.		Fabio Capello	Russian national team	9 m.
7.		André Villas-Boas	Zenit Saint Petersburg	8.5 m.
8.		Sven Goran Eriksson	Shanghai SIPG	8 m.
9.		Jürgen Klopp	Borussia Dortmund	7.2 m.
10.		Laurent Blanc	PSG	7 m.
10.		David Moyes	Real Sociedad San Sebastián	7 m.

meet the 10 most valuable players

The most valuable players in the world as measured by their 2015 transfer market value.

Rank	Nationality	Name	Age	Club	Market value in €	
1	Argentina/Spain	Lionel Messi	28	FC Barcelona	120 m.	
2	Portugal	Cristiano Ronaldo	30	Real Madrid	110 m.	
3	Brazil	Neymar	23	FC Barcelona	100 m.	
4	Uruguay	Luis Suárez	28	FC Barcelona	90 m.	
5	Columbia	James Rodríguez	24	Real Madrid	80 m.	
6	Wales	Gareth Bale	26	Real Madrid	80 m.	
7	Germany	Thomas Müller	26	FC Bayern	75 m.	
8	Belgium	Eden Hazard	24	FC Chelsea	70 m.	
9	Poland	Robert Lewandowski	27	FC Bayern	70 m.	
10	Belgium	Kevin de Bruyne	24	Manchester City	60 m.	

have a look at the most valuable left-backs

The most valuable left-backs in the world as measured by their 2015 market value.

Rank	Nationality	Name	Age	Club	Market value in €	
1	Austria	David Alaba	23	FC Bayern	45 m.	
2	Spain	Jordi Alba	26	FC Barcelona	35 m.	
3	Brazil	Marcelo	27	Real Madrid	30 m.	
4	Switzerland	Ricardo Rodríguez	23	VFL Wolfsburg	28 m.	
5	Brazil	Alex Sandro	24	Juventus Turin	24 m.	
6	Spain	César Azpilcueta	26	FC Chelsea	23 m.	
7	England	Luke Shaw	20	Manchester United	21 m.	
8	Spain	José Luis Gayá	20	FC Valencia	20 m.	
9	Spain	Juan Bernat	22	FC Bayern	20 m.	
10	France	Layvin Kurzawa	23	Paris Saint-Germain	20 m.	

meet the world's 10 best-paid male players

1. Lionel Messi (FC Barcelona): 65 million (annual salary: 36 million, bonuses: 1 million, other: 28 million)

2. Cristiano Ronaldo (Real Madrid): 54 million (annual salary: 27 million, bonuses: 1 million, other: 26 million)

3. Neymar (FC Barcelona): 36.5 million (annual salary: 20 million, bonuses: 500,000, other: 16 million)

4. Thiago Silva (Paris Saint-Germain): 27.5 million (annual salary: 23 million, bonuses: 1 million, other: 3.5 million)

5. Robin van Persie (Manchester United): 25.6 million (annual salary: 16.1 million, bonuses: 7 million, other: 2.5 million)

6. Gareth Bale (Real Madrid): 23.8 million (annual salary: 14 million, bonuses: 800,000, other: 9 million)

7. Wayne Rooney (Manchester United): 22.5 million (annual salary: 16.1 million, bonuses: 200,000, other: 6.2 million)

8. Zlatan Ibrahimovic (Paris Saint-Germain): 21.5 million (annual salary: 15 million, bonuses: 2 million, other: 4.5 million)

9. Sergio Agüero (Manchester City): 21.2 million (annual salary: 14.6 million, bonuses: 600,000, other: 6 million)

10. Robert Lewandowski (FC Bayern): 20.2 million (annual salary: 9 million, bonuses: 10 million, other: 1.2 million)

Annual salary

Bonuses

Other

Effective 2015, in €

As in most professions, there are also income disparities between men and women in sports.

1. Marta Vieira da Silva (FC Rosengård): 460,000

2. Alex Morgan (Portland Thorns FC): 410,000

3. Abby Wambach (Seattle Reign FC): 275,000

4. Sydney Leroux (Western New York Flash): 85,000

5. Nicole Banecki (SC Freiburg): 82,000

6. Amandine Henry (Olympique Lyon): 64,000

7. Nilla Fischer (VfL Wolfsburg): 62,000

8. Hope Solo (Seattle Reign FC): 60,000

9. Jonelle Filigno (Sky Blue FC): 55,000

10. Laure Boulleau (Paris Saint-Germain): 55,000

Effective 2015, in €

Player	Position	Season	Buying club	Transfer fee
1 Gareth Bale	Right-winger	13/14	Real Madrid	100.76 million €
2 Cristiano Ronaldo	Left-winger	09/10	Real Madrid	94 million €
3 Neymar	Left-winger	13/14	FC Barcelona	86.2 million €
4 Luis Suárez	Center-forward	14/15	FC Barcelona	81 million €
5 James Rodríguez	Offensive midfielder	14/15	Real Madrid	80 million €
6 Zinédine Zidane	Offensive midfielder	01/02	Real Madrid	76 million €
7 Ángel Di María	Right-winger	14/15	Manchester Utd.	75 million €
8 Kevin De Bruyne	Offensive midfielder	15/16	Manchester City	75 million €
9 Zlatan Ibrahimovic	Center-forward	09/10	FC Barcelona	70 million €
10 Raheem Sterling	Offensive midfielder	14/15	Manchester City	69 million €

Effective 2015

learn about prize money

Men's World Cup:

The following prize money was awarded at the 2014 World Cup:

- 1. place: Germany: USD 35 million
- 2. place: Argentina: USD 25 million
- 3. place: Netherlands: USD 22 million

Women's World Cup:

The participants of the 2015 World Cup received prize money that was 50% higher than that of 2011,
just as they had at the two preceeding World Cups. The teams of the participating clubs received the following prize money:

- 1. place: USA: USD 2 million
- 2. place: Japan: USD 1.3 million
- 3. place: England: USD 1 million

study the history of defense

50s
Stoppers until ca. 1960

60s
Watchdog until ca. 1970

70s
Terrier until ca. 1980

80s
Center half until ca. 1995

90s
Marker until ca. 2000
Sweeper until ca. 2000

90s–00s
Pure destroyer until ca. 2005

00s–10s
Stopper until today
Full-back until today

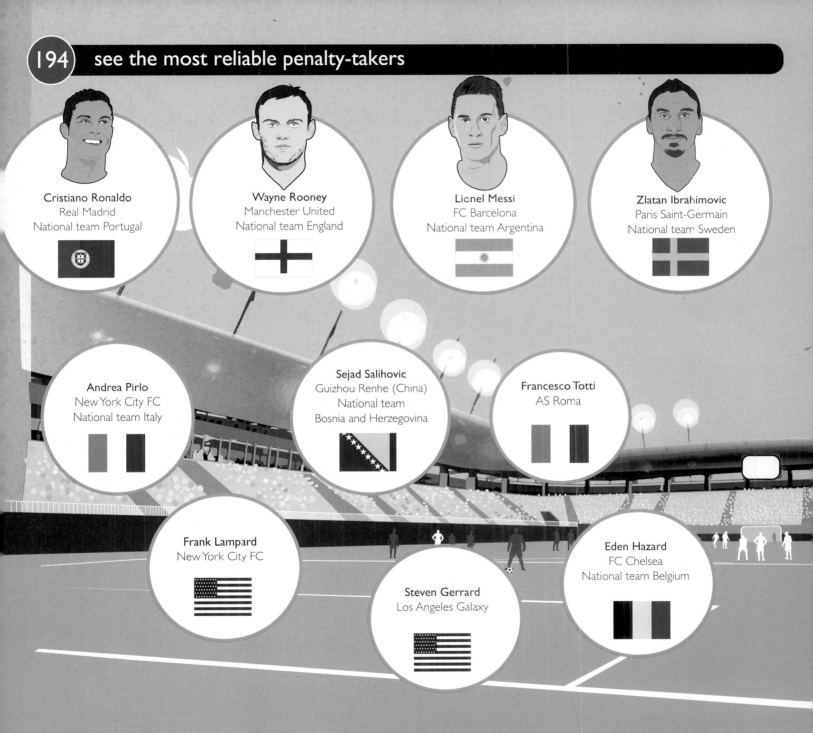

Cristiano Ronaldo
Real Madrid
National team Portugal

Wayne Rooney
Manchester United
National team England

Licnel Messi
FC Barcelona
National team Argentina

Zlatan Ibrahimovic
Paris Saint-Germain
National team Sweden

Andrea Pirlo
New York City FC
National team Italy

Sejad Salihovic
Guizhou Renhe (China)
National team
Bosnia and Herzegovina

Francesco Totti
AS Roma

Frank Lampard
New York City FC

Steven Gerrard
Los Angeles Galaxy

Eden Hazard
FC Chelsea
National team Belgium

Arjen Robben	Zlatan Ibrahimovic	David Beckham	Mark van Bommel	Wesley Sneijder
2003–2015	2002–2015	1996–2013	2000–2011	2004–2013
Champion in:	**Champion in:**	**Champion in:**	**Champion in:**	**Champion in:**
Netherlands	Netherlands	England	Netherlands	Netherlands
England	Italy	Spain	Spain	Spain
Spain	Spain	USA	Germany	Italy
Germany	France	France	Italy	Turkey

Heart rate during a match is usually more than 80% of the overall maximum.

A player runs about 6.2–9.3 mi / 0–13 km per match, including about 0.6–0.9 mi / 1–1.5 km of sprints and 1,970 ft / 600 m in backward movement.

Calories burned: about 1,600 cal per match

The injury rate is highest for strikers.

The most shots

1. Karim Benzema (France) 32 shots in 450 minutes

2. Angel di Maria (Argentina) 25 shots in 423 minutes

3. Cristiano Ronaldo (Portugal) 23 shots in 270 minutes

4. Lionel Messi (Argentina) 22 shots in 693 minutes

The most passes

1. Philipp Lahm (Germany) 651 passes in 690 minutes

2. Toni Kroos (Germany) 633 passes in 690 minutes

3. Javier Mascherano (Argentina) 626 passes in 720 minutes

The most distance run

1. Thomas Müller (Germany) 52.2 miles / 84.0 km in 682 minutes

2. Toni Kroos (Germany) 51.3 miles / 82.6 km in 650 minutes

3. Javier Mascherano (Argentina) 50.5 miles / 81.2 km in 720 minutes

Castrol Index (FIFA Index) Brazil 2014

Castrol, official sponsor of the World Cup in Brazil, uses the same expertise and data analysis applied to studying lubricants to evaluate players' perfomances. All passes, tackles, and movements on the playing field are recorded and evaluated.

Ranking of the players according to the Castrol Index:

1. Toni Kroos

2. Arjen Robben

3. Stefan de Vrij

4. Mats Hummels

5. Thomas Müller

6. Karim Benzema

7. Oscar

8. Thiago Silva

9. Marcos Rojo

10. Ron Vlaar

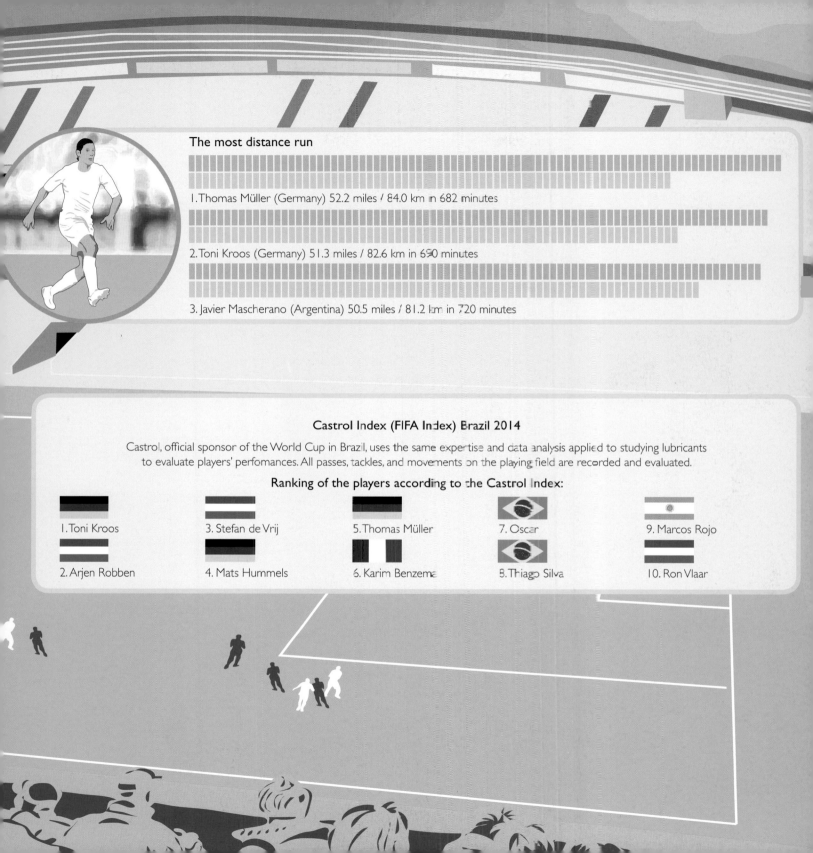

After his winning goals against Chelsea in 2000 Thierry Henry (Arsenal London) ran into the corner flag with his face, and had to be treated by the team doctor.

Paolo Diogo got his wedding ring stuck in the fence while celebrating at the stands. He lost half his finger and was given a yellow card for "celebrating too excessively."

Volkan Demirel (Fenerbahçe Istanbul) flung his shirt into the stands after the game ended and dislocated his shoulder doing so.

Martin Palermo (FC Villarreal) was cheering on top of a wall above the goal. The wall caved in—and so did his left leg!

Adam Nemec (1. FC Kaiserslautern) fell from a tree, suffering a concussion and fracturing two thoracic vertebrae and his collarbone.

Kasey Keller (FC Millwall) took his golf clubs out of the trunk and knocked his front teeth out.

Markus Pröll (Eintracht Frankfurt) toppled over a small girl—dislocating his shoulder in the process.

Darren Barnard (FC Barnsley) slipped in the kitchen on a puppy's puddle of urine—resulting in torn knee ligaments and five months' rest.

Ewald Lienen (Arminia Bielefeld): suffered a 10-in / 25-cm long, 2-in / 5-cm deep cut to his thigh during a tackle in 1981.

Franz Michelberger (FC Bayern): A camel rammed him against the team bus in the training camp in Israel, injuring his knee.

Marco Arnautović (Werder Bremen) Was playing with his dog and twisted his knee, tearing the medial collateral ligaments.

Jérôme Boateng (FC Bayern): After injuring his knee in the World Cup, a flight attendant aggravated the injury by bumping it with a drinks cart.

Éver Banega (FC Valencia) was fueling his car, which started to move. He tried to stop it, earning a broken foot and six months' rest.

Robbie Keane (Wolverhampton Wanderers) was lying on the sofa, fishing for the remote control with his foot—and ruptured cartilage in his knee.

Since 1991, FIFA has awarded the title "World Players of the Year" to male players. In 2010, it was consolidated with the "Ballon d'Or" prize of the French soccer magazine *France Football* and became the FIFA Ballon d'Or. In 2013, Pelé received the FIFA Ballon d'Or Prix d'Honneur in recognition of his lifetime achievements.

Players

Men

Year	Player	Nationality	Club
2015	Lionel Messi	Brazil	Real Madrid
2014	Cristiano Ronaldo	Portugal	Real Madrid
2013	Cristiano Ronaldo	Portugal	Real Madrid
2012	Lionel Messi	Argentina	FC Barcelona
2011	Lionel Messi	Argentina	FC Barcelona
2010	Lionel Messi	Argentina	FC Barcelona
2009	Lionel Messi	Argentina	FC Barcelona
2008	Cristiano Ronaldo	Portugal	Manchester United
2007	Kaká	Brazil	AC Milan
2006	Fabio Cannavaro	Italy	Juventus Turin, Real Madrid
2005	Ronaldinho	Brazil	FC Barcelona
2004	Ronaldinho	Brazil	FC Barcelona
2003	Zinédine Zidane	France	Real Madrid
2002	Ronaldo	Brazil	Inter Milan, Real Madrid
2001	Luís Figo	Portugal	Real Madrid
2000	Zinédine Zidane	France	Juventus Turin
1999	Rivaldo	Brazil	FC Barcelona
1998	Zinédine Zidane	France	Juventus Turin
1997	Ronaldo	Brazil	FC Barcelona, Inter Milan
1996	Ronaldo	Brazil	PSV Eindhoven, FC Barcelona
1995	George Weah	Liberia	Paris Saint-Germain, AC Milan
1994	Romário	Brazil	FC Barcelona
1993	Roberto Baggio	Italy	Juventus Turin
1992	Marco van Basten	Netherlands	AC Milan
1991	Lothar Matthäus	Germany	Inter Milan

Trainers

Men

Year	Name	Nationality	Team
2015	Luis Enrique	Spain	FC Barcelona
2014	Joachim Löw	Germany	Germany
2013	Jupp Heynckes	Germany	FC Bayern
2012	Vicente del Bosque	Spain	Spain
2011	Pep Guardiola	Spain	FC Barcelona
2010	José Mourinho	Portugal	Inter Milan/Real Madrid

Since 2001, FIFA has also awarded "World Player of the Year" to women.

Players

Year	Player	Women Nationality	Club
2015	Carli Lloyd	USA	Houston Dash
2014	Nadine Kessler	Germany	VfL Wolfsburg
2013	Nadine Angerer	Germany	I. FFC Frankfurt Brisbane Roar
2012	Abby Wambach	USA	no affiliation
2011	Homare Sawa	Japan	INAC Kobe Leonessa
2010	Marta	Brazil	FC Gold Pride
2009	Marta	Brazil	Los Angeles Sol
2008	Marta	Brazil	Umeå IK
2007	Marta	Brazil	Umeå IK
2006	Marta	Brazil	Umeå IK
2005	Birgit Prinz	Germany	I. FFC Frankfurt
2004	Birgit Prinz	Germany	I. FFC Frankfurt
2003	Birgit Prinz	Germany	I. FFC Frankfurt
2002	Mia Hamm	USA	Washington Freedom
2001	Mia Hamm	USA	Washington Freedom

The prize "FIFA Trainer of the Year" has only been awarded
since 2010 in the context of the FIFA Ballon d'Or.

Trainers

Year	Name	Women Nationality	Team
2015	Jill Ellis	USA	USA
2014	Ralf Kellermann	Germany	VfL Wolfsburg
2013	Silvia Neid	Germany	Germany
2012	Pia Sundhage	Sweden	USA
2011	Norio Sasaki	Japan	Japan
2010	Silvia Neid	Germany	Germany

Karl "Calle" Del'Haye
National team
Germany

Souleymane Sanè
National team
Senegal

Carlos Valderrama
National team
Columbia

Norbert Dronia
Former German
soccer player

Stefan Effenberg (back of head)
National team
Germany

Alain Sutter
National team
Switzerland

Manuel Antonio Morais
"Locô" Cange
National team
Angola

Ratinho
Former Brazilian soccer
player

Mike Werner
Former
German soccer
player

In Italian, the mullet is called "capelli alla tedesca" (German-style hair),
in Dutch "duitse mat" (German mop), and in Hungarian "Bundesliga".

Karen Carney
National team
England

Celia Sasic
National team
Germany

Sophie Schmidt
National team
Canada

Gaëlle Enganamouit
National team
Cameroon

Karina LeBlanc
National team
Canada

Jeon Ga-eul
National team
South Korea

1. When is an outfield player allowed to take the goalkeeper's position?

2. What do Lionel Messi's fans call him?

3. What is a passive offside?

4. Which fan item is constantly being debated to be considered forbidden for stadiums?

8. Which soccer player is called "the non-flying dutchman"?

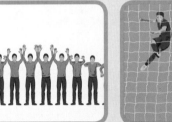

9. At what speed does the Mexican wave move across the stadium?

10. What is the away goal rule?

11. Which soccer club has the most spectators overall?

15. What is the inofficial hymn of the Italian national team?

16. Which sports division has the most spectators?

17. What do you call a ball that jumps straight up?

18. What is a Rabona?

Score: For each correct answer you get one point.

0-5 points: You should read the book again!

6-13 points: The book has made you wiser and more knowledgeable; buy another one and give it away as a present.

14-20 points: You are a true soccer lover; you can look forward to the second edition.

21-25 points: Seriously! Admit it! You cheated and looked at the answers!

22. What is the name of the best paid female soccer player?

5. When was the first women's soccer team founded?

6. How does a linesman signal a substitution?

7. What is the name of the first FIFA president?

12. When was goalline technology authorized?

13. What is CONCACAF?

14. What is the 2-3-5 pyramid formation?

19. Who scored the first World Cup goal?

20. Which formation did Inter Milan use in the 1960s?

21. What year did Brazil become world champion?

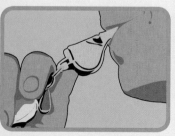

23. Which referee whistled in the most World Cup matches?

24. Who was the inventor of the yellow and red cards?

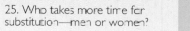

25. Who takes more time for substitution—men or women?

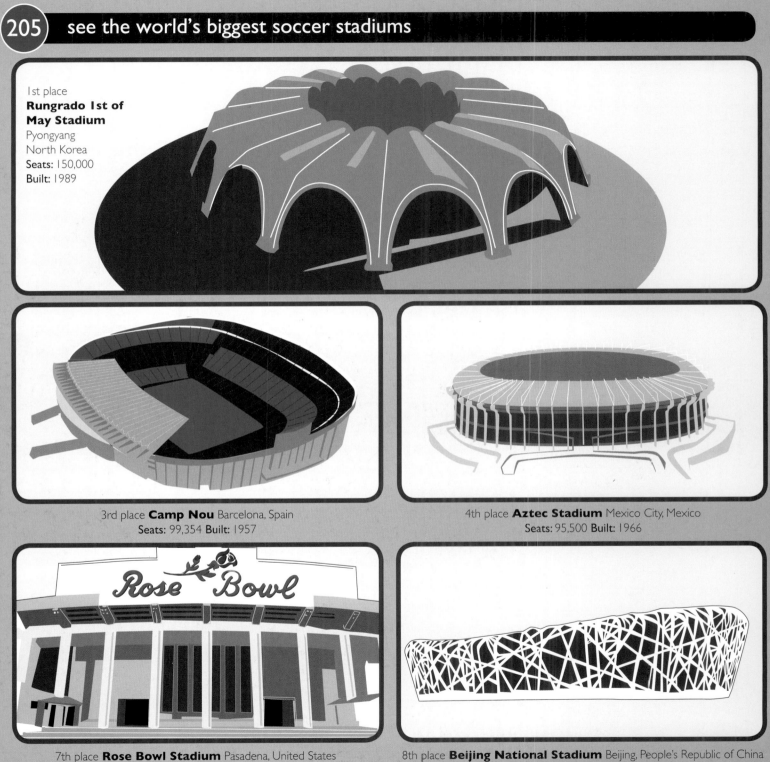

1st place
Rungrado 1st of May Stadium
Pyongyang
North Korea
Seats: 150,000
Built: 1989

3rd place **Camp Nou** Barcelona, Spain
Seats: 99,354 **Built:** 1957

4th place **Aztec Stadium** Mexico City, Mexico
Seats: 95,500 **Built:** 1966

7th place **Rose Bowl Stadium** Pasadena, United States
Seats: 91,136 **Built:** 1923

8th place **Beijing National Stadium** Beijing, People's Republic of China
Seats: 91,000 **Built:** 2008

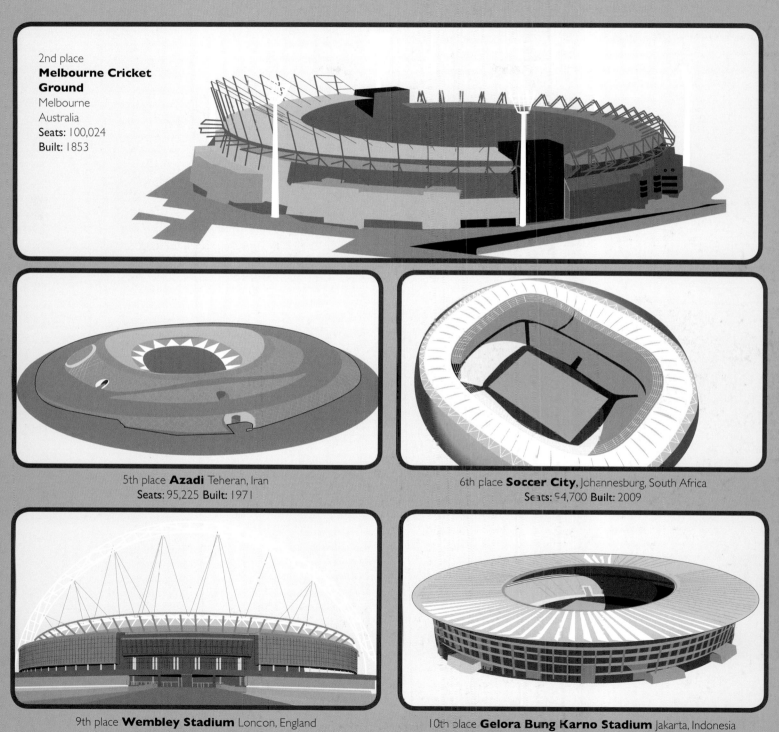

2nd place
Melbourne Cricket Ground
Melbourne
Australia
Seats: 100,024
Built: 1853

5th place **Azadi** Teheran, Iran
Seats: 95,225 Built: 1971

6th place **Soccer City,** Johannesburg, South Africa
Seats: 94,700 Built: 2009

9th place **Wembley Stadium** London, England
Seats: 90,000 Built: 2007

10th place **Gelora Bung Karno Stadium** Jakarta, Indonesia
Seats: 88,306 Built: 1962

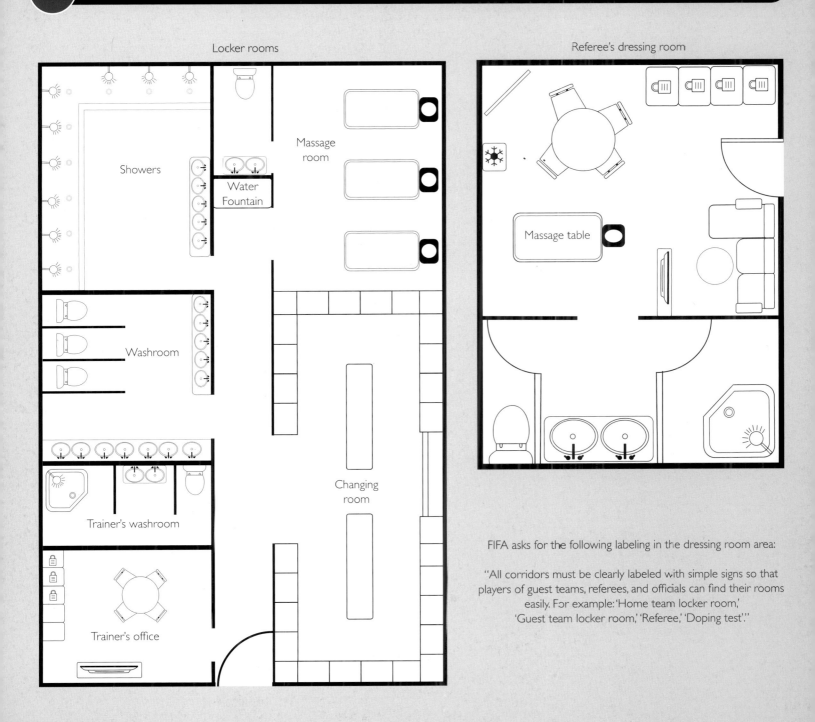

Locker rooms

Showers

Water Fountain

Massage room

Washroom

Trainer's washroom

Trainer's office

Changing room

Referee's dressing room

Massage table

FIFA asks for the following labeling in the dressing room area:

"All corridors must be clearly labeled with simple signs so that players of guest teams, referees, and officials can find their rooms easily. For example:'Home team locker room,' 'Guest team locker room,' 'Referee,' 'Doping test'."

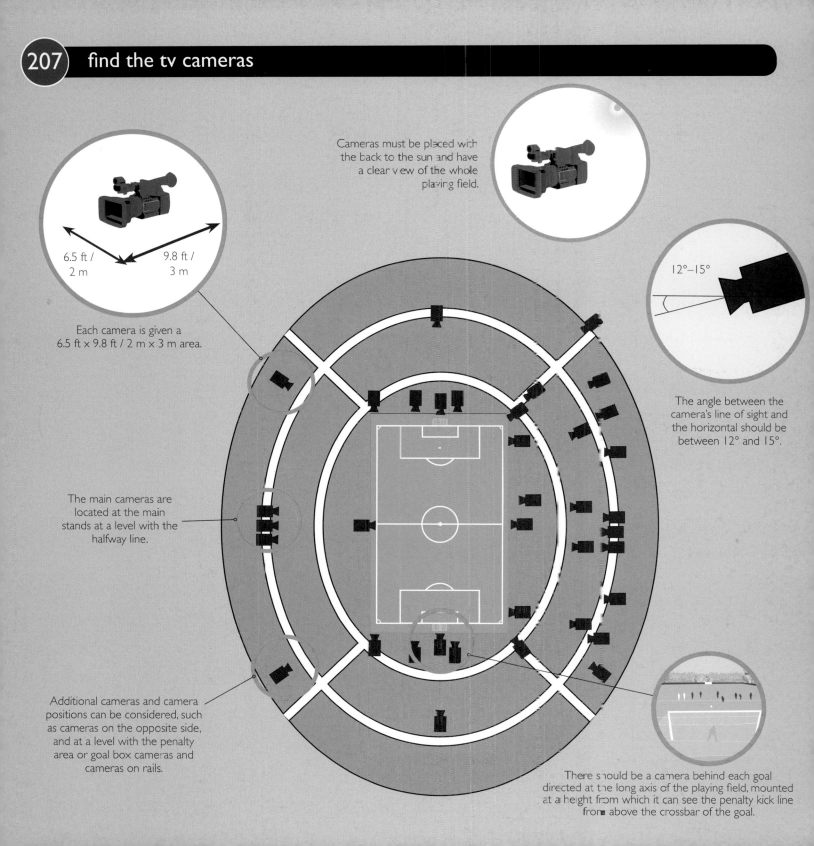

Cameras must be placed with the back to the sun and have a clear view of the whole playing field.

6.5 ft / 2 m   9.8 ft / 3 m

Each camera is given a 6.5 ft × 9.8 ft / 2 m × 3 m area.

12°–15°

The angle between the camera's line of sight and the horizontal should be between 12° and 15°.

The main cameras are located at the main stands at a level with the halfway line.

Additional cameras and camera positions can be considered, such as cameras on the opposite side, and at a level with the penalty area or goal box cameras and cameras on rails.

There should be a camera behind each goal directed at the long axis of the playing field, mounted at a height from which it can see the penalty kick line from above the crossbar of the goal.

208   learn about the longest matches

The longest soccer match of all time ended after 35 hours and more than 600 goals. 333-293 was the score of a charity match between the Cotswold All Stars and the Cambray FC in England. However, amateur teams broke this record in another charity match: They played for 73 hours; the match ended 475-473.

209   break this ball-handling record

The Ukrainian Nikolai Kutsenko is the absolute record holder. In 1995 he held the ball up with his head and feet for 24 hours and 30 minutes, without any breaks and without letting the ball touch the ground.

210   keep up with these keep-ups

On December 12th, 2006, in Victoria, British Columbia, Canada, ten-year-old Chloe Hegland kept the ball bouncing on her foot, 155 times in 30 seconds.

211   review this record defeat

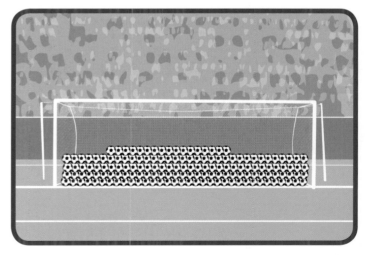

In Madagascar the team of Stade Olympique l'Emyrne protested against the referee by scoring 149 own goals and set a record. The beneficiary was the club AS Adema.

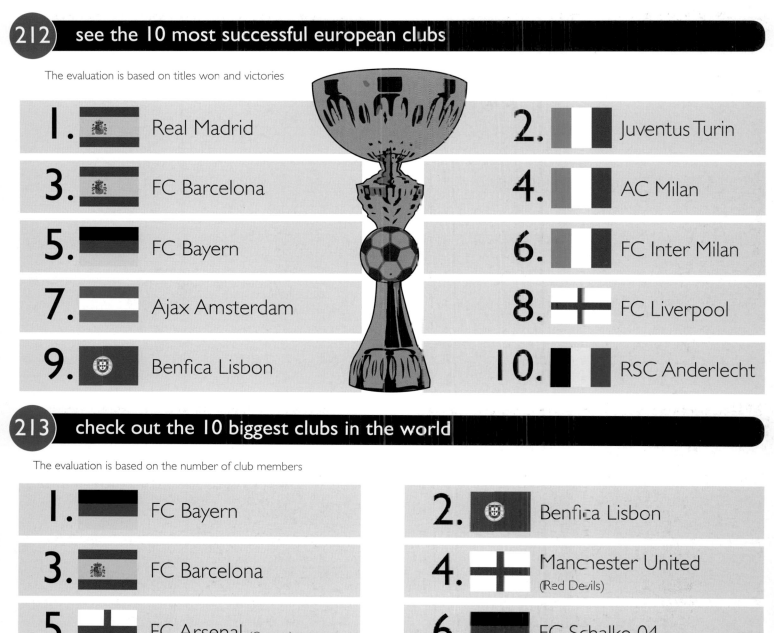

212   see the 10 most successful european clubs

The evaluation is based on titles won and victories

1. Real Madrid

2. Juventus Turin

3. FC Barcelona

4. AC Milan

5. FC Bayern

6. FC Inter Milan

7. Ajax Amsterdam

8. FC Liverpool

9. Benfica Lisbon

10. RSC Anderlecht

213   check out the 10 biggest clubs in the world

The evaluation is based on the number of club members

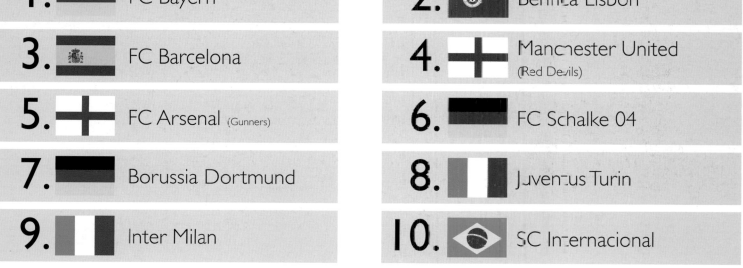

1. FC Bayern

2. Benfica Lisbon

3. FC Barcelona

4. Manchester United (Red Devils)

5. FC Arsenal (Gunners)

6. FC Schalke 04

7. Borussia Dortmund

8. Juventus Turin

9. Inter Milan

10. SC Internacional

This game is only played on sand at the Piazza Santa Croce in Florence.

The final takes place on June 24th, on the saint's day of John the Baptist, the patron saint of Florence.

The calcio storico is played with four teams: The azzurri are from the district Santa Croce, the rossi from Santa Maria Novella, the bianchi from Santo Spirito, and the verdi from Santo Giovanni. 27 men each play against each other.

The ball can be played with every body part. Beating, kicking, and wrestling are allowed.

The match lasts 50 minutes; it's interrupted only for paramedics who need to evacuate injured players.
Ball in the net: The team scores a point.
Ball over the net: The opposing team scores half a point.

This game is played on Orkney Island, Scotland, at Christmas and New Year's. Place of birth determines who plays for which team.

Uppies—Southern part of the town.

Doonies—Northern part of the town.

Kickoff: 1 p.m.

The entire town is the playing area.

The uppie goal is an exterior wall of a house; the doonie goal is the dock.

The number of players is unlimited and there are hardly any fixed rules.

take part in the clericus cup

World Cup of the Vatican

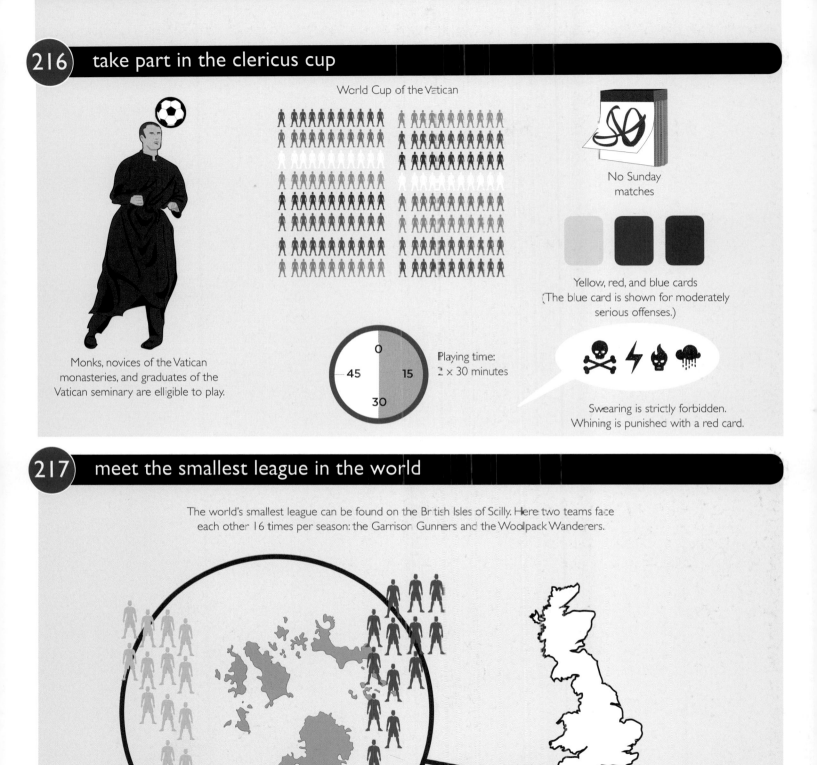

Monks, novices of the Vatican monasteries, and graduates of the Vatican seminary are elligible to play.

No Sunday matches

Yellow, red, and blue cards
(The blue card is shown for moderately serious offenses.)

Playing time:
2 x 30 minutes

Swearing is strictly forbidden.
Whining is punished with a red card.

meet the smallest league in the world

The world's smallest league can be found on the British Isles of Scilly. Here two teams face each other 16 times per season: the Garrison Gunners and the Woolpack Wanderers.

Iker Casillas doesn't take off his goalkeeper gloves to sign autographs, and ties two fingers together for each game.

Cristiano Ronaldo pulls up his socks as high as possible.

Luís Figo allegedly ran over a black cat in order to ward of bad luck for his team.

David Beckham plays with the shirt number 23 or 7.

Franck Ribéry prays before each game.

Mario Gomez never sings along with the national anthem and always chooses the left urinal.

Raymond Domenech, former French national trainer, is said to have positioned his players according to their zodiac signs.

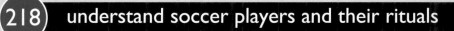

Like many others, Giuseppe Rossi touches the ceiling of the tunnel when taking to the field.

learn about the biggest local rivals

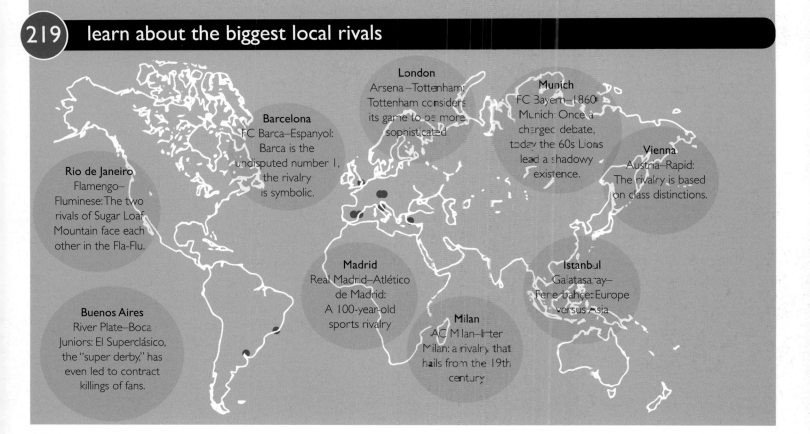

London
Arsenal–Tottenham: Tottenham considers its game to be more sophisticated

Munich
FC Bayern–1860 Munich: Once a charged debate, today the 60s Lions lead a shadowy existence.

Barcelona
FC Barca–Espanyol: Barca is the undisputed number 1, the rivalry is symbolic.

Vienna
Austria–Rapid: The rivalry is based on class distinctions.

Rio de Janeiro
Flamengo–Fluminese: The two rivals of Sugar Loaf Mountain face each other in the Fla-Flu.

Madrid
Real Madrid–Atlético de Madrid: A 100-year-old sports rivalry

Istanbul
Galatasaray–Fenerbahçe: Europe versus Asia

Buenos Aires
River Plate–Boca Juniors: El Superclásico, the "super derby," has even led to contract killings of fans.

Milan
AC Milan–Inter Milan: a rivalry that hails from the 19th century

see soccer players' other jobs

Fabian Boll: Detective chief inspector

Miroslav Klose: Carpenter by trade

Alexi Lalas: Rock musician

Jonathan de Falco: Porn star

Tomas Brolin: Singer, vacuum cleaner salesman, model

Robbie Fowler: Racehorse owner and realtor

Lothar Matthäus: Interior decorater by trade

Ken Monkou: Owner of a pancake house

Giovanni Trapattoni: Since 2010 national trainer of Vatican City

Curtis Woodhouse: Boxer

Cristiano Ronaldo: Owner of a hotel chain (CR7)

Juliar Dicks: Golf player, dog breeder, pub owner

Arjan de Zeeuw: Private detective

Bixente Lizarazu: Jiujitsu fighter

Index

References are to item numbers, not to page numbers.

weldon**owen**

1045 Sansome Street, San Francisco, California, USA
www.weldonowen.com

THE COMPLETE QUICK-LOOK GUIDE
TO THE GAME OF SOCCER

A WELDON OWEN PRODUCTION

Copyright © 2016 Weldon Owen, Inc.
All rights reserved, including the right of reproduction
in whole or in part in any form.

Printed in China by 1010 Printing international

First printed in 2016
10 9 8 7 6 5 4 3 2 1

Library of Congress Control Number, on file with the publisher

ISBN 13: 978-1-68188-111-9
ISBN 10: 1-68188-111-X

Weldon Owen is a division of Bonnier Publishing

WELDON OWEN, INC.

President & Publisher Roger Shaw
SVP, Sales & Marketing Amy Kaneko
Finance Director Philip Paulick

Creative Director Kelly Booth
Cover Designer Debbie Berne
Senior Production Designer Rachel Lopez Metzger

Associate Publisher Mariah Bear
Associate Editor Ian Cannon
With editorial assitance from Molly Stewart;
index by Kevin Broccoli of BIM Creatives, LLC

Production Director Chris Hemesath
Associate Production Director Michelle Duggan

Author Gabriela Scolik
Illustrations Karin Dreher
Team Bettina Dietrich,
Daniela Schmid, Norbert Wurzinger
Translation Katharine Apostle

SHOW ME NOW™

A Show Me Now Book.
Show Me Now is a trademark
of Weldon Owen Inc.
www.showmenow.com